ALBERTO GIACOMETTI

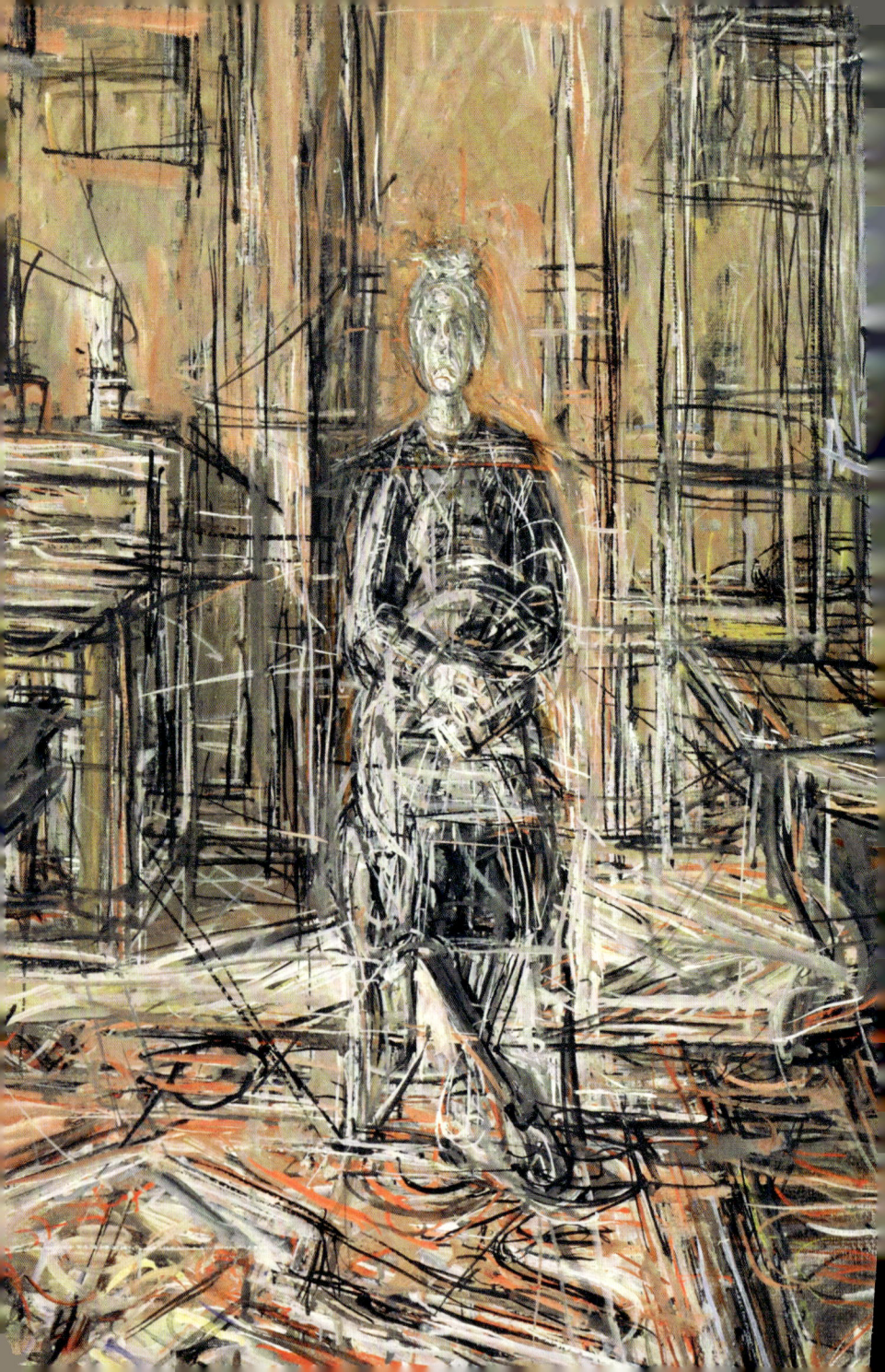

ALBERTO GIACOMETTI

LENA FRITSCH

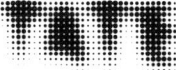

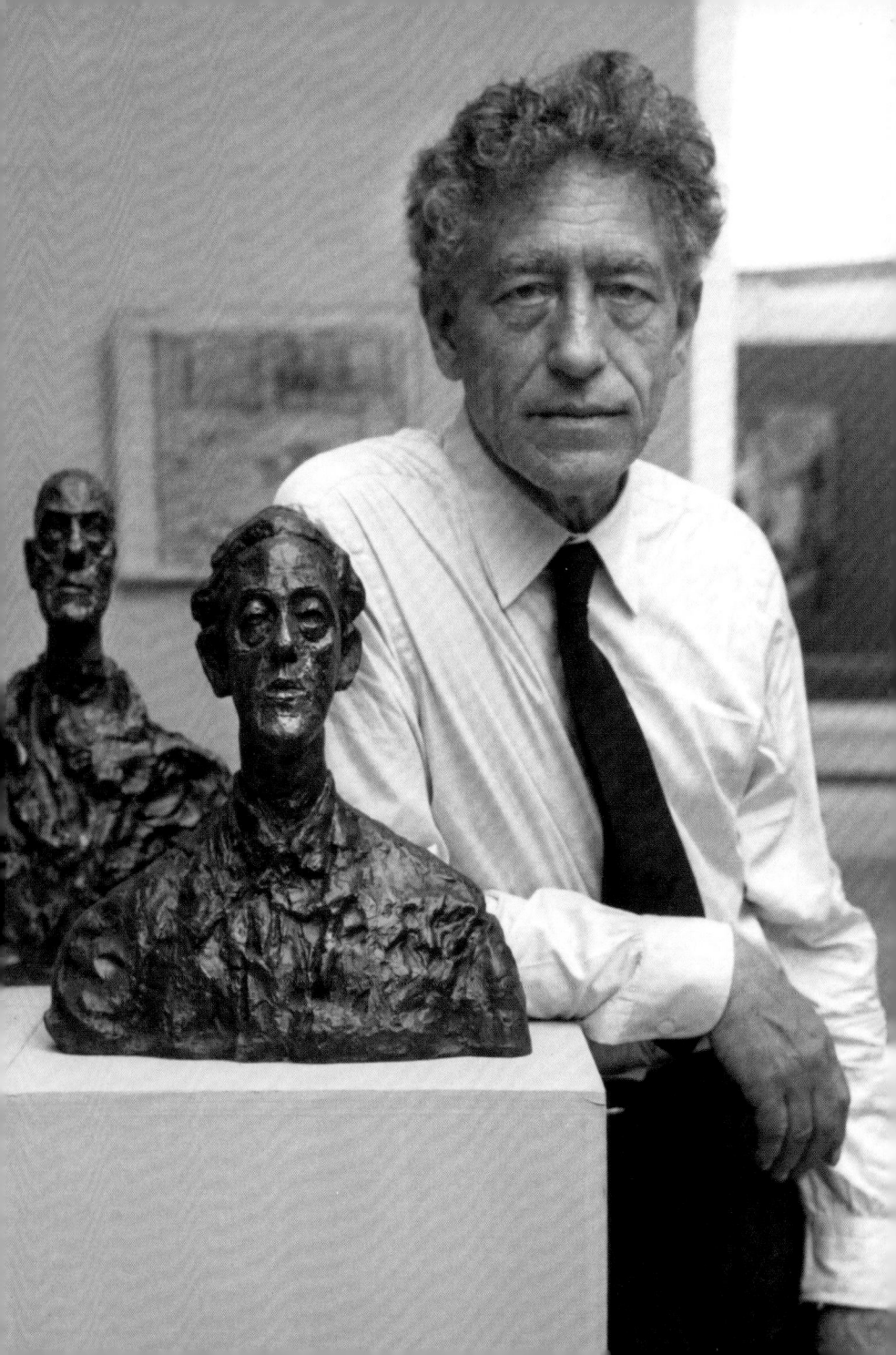

There was no greater pleasure for me than to run into the studio after school and sit in my corner by the window to look at books and draw … Of course I was very much influenced by my father, but I was attracted almost as much by the illustrations of paintings I discovered in books.[1]

Alberto Giacometti was born on 10 October 1901 in the village of Borgonovo in the Italian-speaking valley of Bregaglia in the mountainous canton of Grisons, Switzerland. He was the first child of Giovanni Giacometti, a well-known painter of post-impressionist works, and Annetta Giacometti-Stampa, who came from one of the valley's wealthiest families. In 1902, his brother Diego was born, followed by their sister Ottilia in 1904 and brother Bruno in 1907.

In 1906, the Giacometti family moved to a house nearby, in the village of Stampa. Giovanni converted the hayloft of a stable into his studio. In a letter to his painter friend and Alberto's godfather Cuno Amiet, Giovanni wrote: 'Perhaps you remember the red house in Stampa … We have decided to move in. The stable will become a very beautiful studio.'[2] Surrounded by his father's paintings, books and art journals, Giacometti began to make drawings in pencil and watercolour. These included self-portraits (p.6), portraits of his family and drawings of his native valley, as well as Bible scenes. Around 1915, Giacometti created his first oil painting: a still life with apples on a table. He also made copies of art that he saw reproduced in his father's books and magazines, for example by Renaissance artist Albrecht Dürer. Throughout his life, Giacometti continued to look at art from the past. He emphasised the pleasure he took in copying reproductions of works of art from different cultures: 'All these copies … are such an important part of my life, of all my activities since my earliest childhood.'[3]

In 1919, Giacometti moved to Geneva to study painting at the École des Beaux-Arts and sculpture at the École des Arts Industriels. In a letter to Amiet he wrote: 'School didn't suit me at first, and then I felt myself very much a stranger in the life of this city, which I find quite cheerful now.'[4] He returned to Stampa in 1920, painting and sculpting in his father's studio. His early watercolours and paintings, for example the portrait *Diego* c.1920 (p.33), were inspired by his father's colourful post-impressionist style.

Giacometti with his works at the Venice Biennale 1962

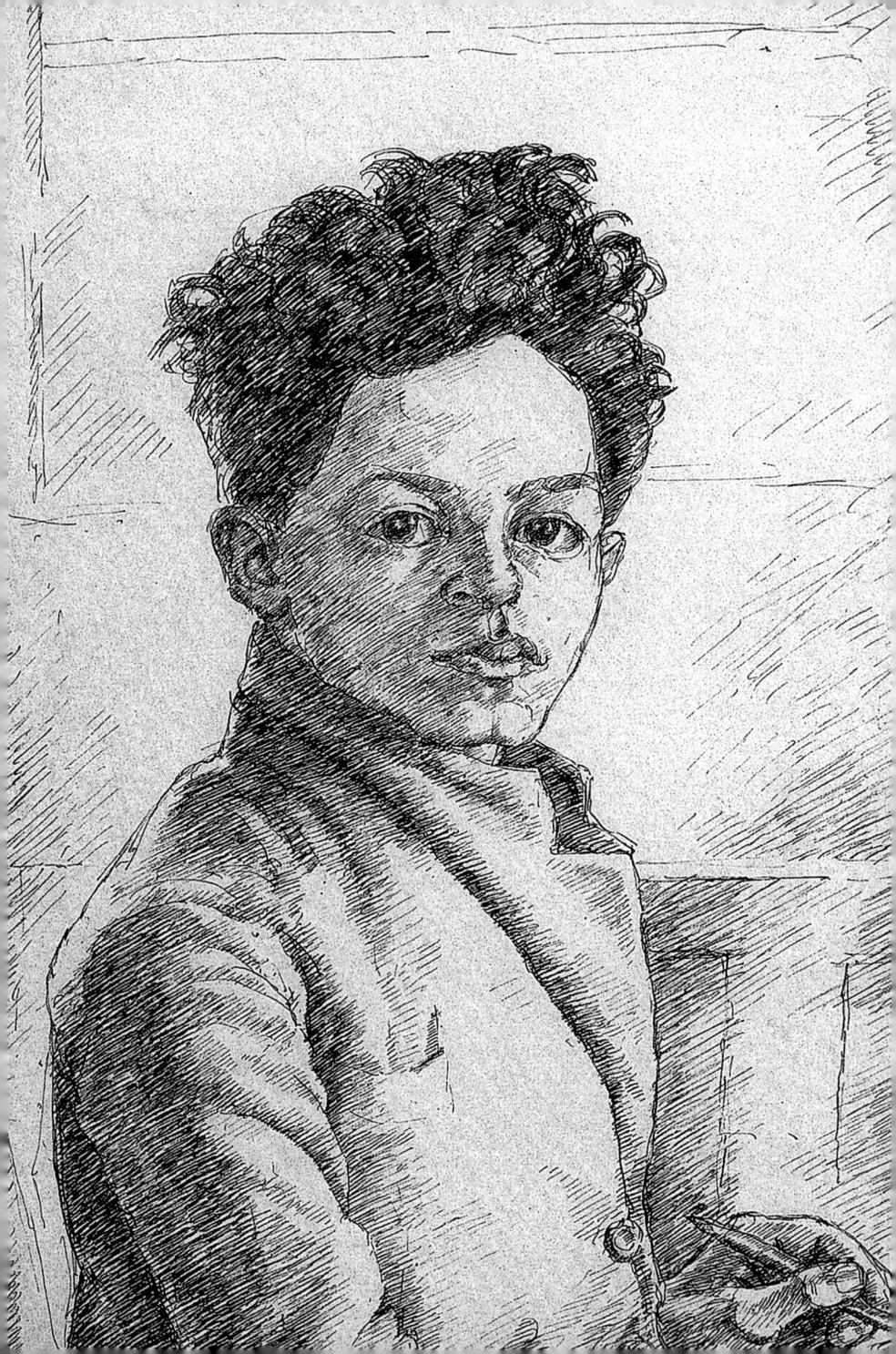

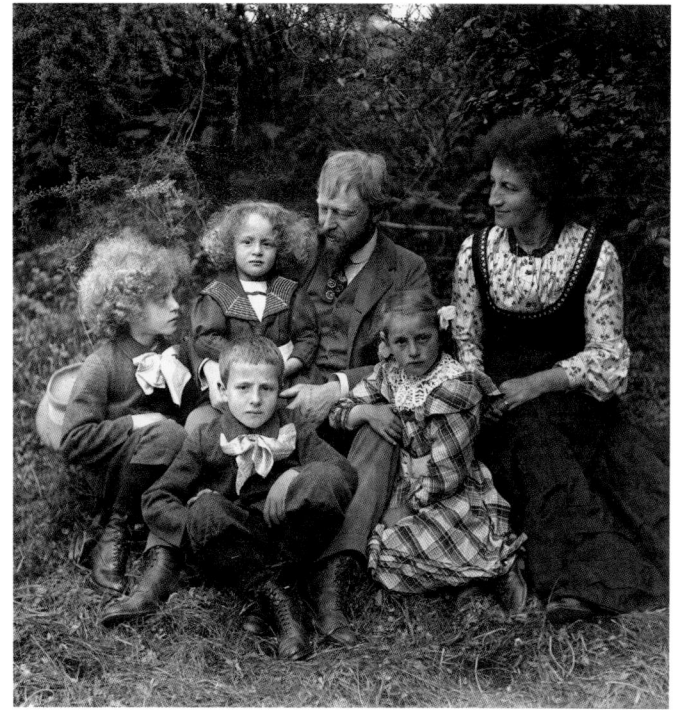

TRAVELS TO ITALY

I stayed nine months in Rome where I could never find enough time to do everything I wanted … I spent a great deal of time in museums, churches, and ruins. I was particularly attracted by mosaics and the Baroque period.[5]

Giovanni Giacometti was a member of the Swiss Federal Art Commission and involved in installing the Swiss section of the Venice Biennale in 1920. He decided to take his son Alberto with him to Italy. The young man was captivated by the works of Renaissance painter Jacopo Tintoretto and the frescoes in the Scrovegni Chapel in Padua by Giotto di Bondone. Travelling to Florence, Perugia, Assisi and Rome in the autumn, he visited museums and churches, studying works of art from Europe as well as from other cultures, particularly ancient Egypt (p.8). He stayed with extended family in Rome and wrote to his parents about his fascination with Egyptian art: 'The Egyptian sculptures are tremendous, their lines and forms are so well-proportioned, their technique is perfect, no-one has ever equalled them.'[6]

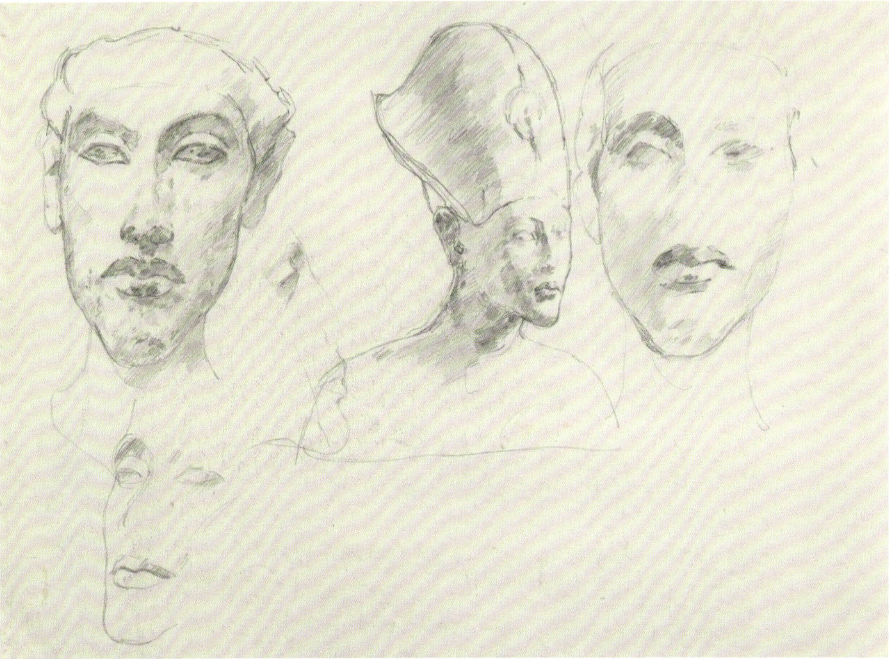

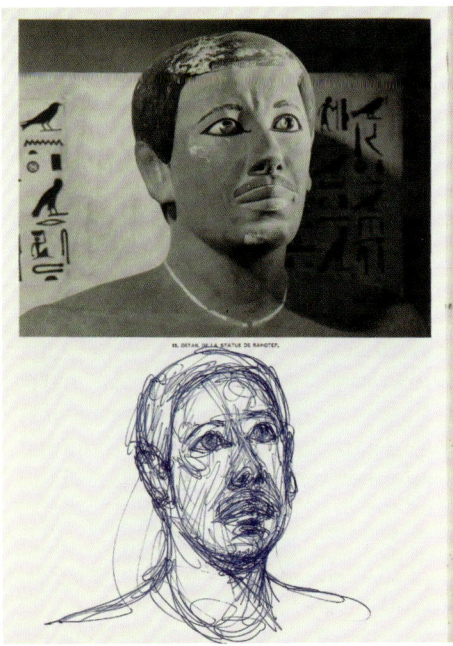

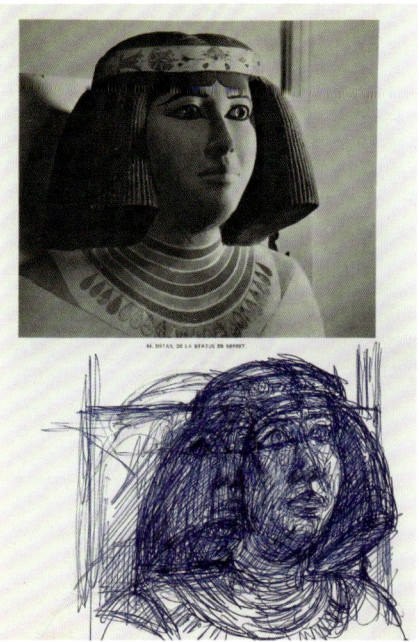

During travels in the following year, Giacometti met the state archivist of The Hague, Pieter van Meurs. At his invitation, the two men began to travel together through the Tyrol to Venice. However, sixty-one-year-old van Meurs was soon taken ill and died in a hotel in Madonna di Campiglio, witnessed by his young companion. Giacometti recollected this early traumatising experience of death in 1963: 'In a few hours Van M. had turned into an object. A nothing. That meant, of course, that death could come at any moment, to me, to the others … My life changed on that day, and I'm not exaggerating … All that started to fall apart for me when I was twenty.'[7] The subject of death and the transformation of the living body into a motionless corpse was to play an important role in different stages of Giacometti's career, as reflected in sculptures such as *Head-Skull* 1934 (p.52) and *The Nose* 1947 (p.58), or the drawing *Braque on His Death Bed* 1963. He also wrote about the experience in his text 'The Dream, the Sphinx, and the Death of T' (1947).

Back in Stampa, Giacometti continued to work in his father's studio. He gradually came to the decision to become a sculptor.

EARLY YEARS IN PARIS & THE STUDIO

I noticed that my way of seeing changed every day.[8]

Giovanni Giacometti had studied fine art in Paris and suggested to his talented son to do the same. Giacometti originally preferred Vienna as the city appeared more entertaining. However, in 1922 he moved to Paris, enrolling in the class of sculptor Antoine Bourdelle at the Académie de la Grande Chaumière. He rented a studio in the artists' quarter of Montparnasse and attended the Académie until 1926, although at times he stayed away for months. He later described his studies with Bourdelle: 'We had to do full-length figure studies after the model. I noticed that my way of seeing changed every day. I would either see a volume or the figure as a patch, either a detail or the whole.'[9]

To make room in his studio, and deeming his early works experimental, Giacometti later destroyed the sculptures that he created during these years.

At the Académie, Giacometti met American fellow student Flora Mayo and began a relationship with her that lasted until 1929. A painted plaster head entitled *Head of a Woman [Flora Mayo]* 1926 (p.34) reflects his girlfriend's features in a stylised way: Giacometti roughly scratched into the flat facial matrix as if it were an etching.

In December 1926 Giacometti moved into a studio building at 46 rue Hippolyte-Maindron. The studio measured 4.75 by 4.90 metres and had high ceilings. There was a shared water tap and toilet in the courtyard. Lacking any comfort but a familiar environment, Giacometti kept the studio until his death. Increasingly crammed with his sculptures and paintings, this picture-perfect context was to become the most popular setting for photographs of Giacometti, taken by almost every big name in photography in the twentieth century, ranging from Paris-based photographers Brassaï and Henri Cartier-Bresson to the Americans Gordon Parks and Alexander Liberman, as well as Swiss photographers Ernst Scheidegger, Herbert Matter and Sabine Weiss. Over the years it acquired a mythical status in the accounts of its visitors.

POST-CUBISM

I began to work at home from memory. This provided – after a number of attempts that bordered on cubism, one necessarily had to touch on it ... – objects that were for me the closest to my vision of reality.[10]

Artists such as Constantin Brâncuşi and Henri Laurens created significant sculptural works by drawing on cubism and the abstraction of non-European tribal art. Their work and African and Oceanic objects now served as a source of inspiration for Giacometti. His sculptures began to show a transition from naturalistic to more abstract forms, as is evident in *Cubist Figure I* c.1926 (p.35). In 1927, the Salon des Tuileries exhibited his sculptures *The Couple* 1927 (p.38) and *Spoon Woman* 1927 (p.39), together with works by Brâncuşi and Ossip Zadkine. *Spoon Woman* is a large figure suggestive of ceremonial spoons from the Dan culture of West Africa. These spoons are associated with festivals and honour women for their generosity, acting as status symbols. The large oval of *Spoon Woman* recalls fertility idols and conveys a spiritual significance. Like many of Giacometti's sculptures, it exists in plaster and in bronze, which was cast later.

Giacometti investigated the motif of the head, continuously reducing all details. The heads, originally based on his father and brother, became increasingly flat and eventually led to the rectangular 'plaque' sculpture *Gazing Head* 1929. The work exists in different materials: plaster, terracotta (p.41) and a

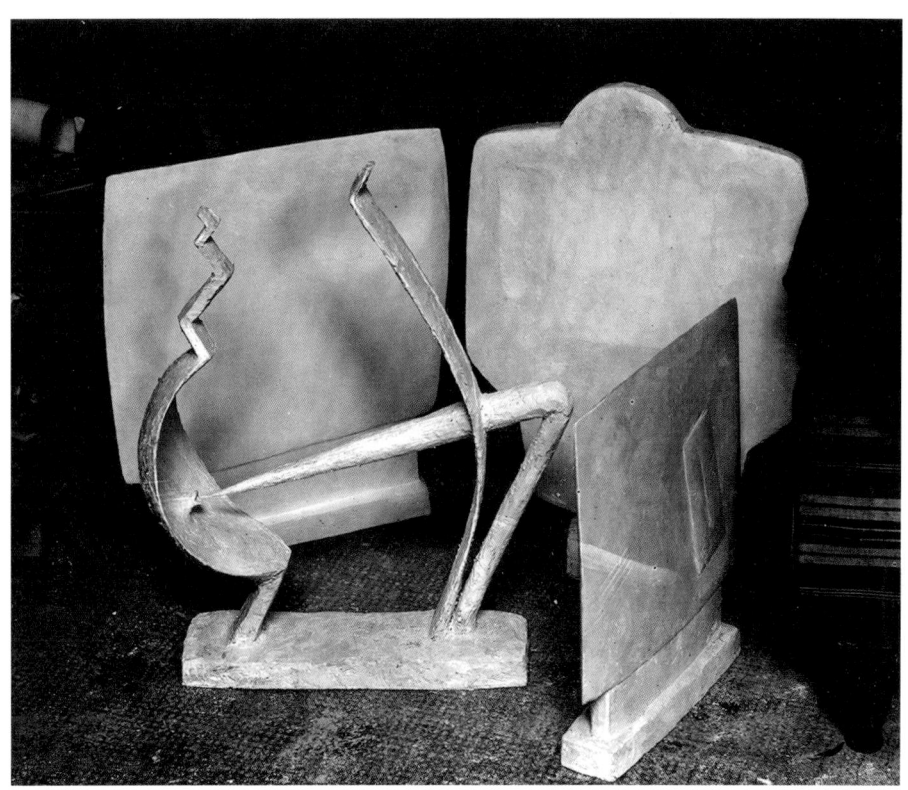

marble version that was executed by his brother Diego, who had first come to Paris in 1925. Giacometti described the working process: 'I began to model from memory as much as possible of what I'd seen ... To get closer to my idea, I had to sacrifice more and more, limit myself – leave off the head, the arms, everything. So what was left of the figure was only a plaque.'[11] While interested in flatness and abstraction, Giacometti also continued to produce more naturalistic heads, for example of his father, when going home to Stampa. Two plaster works exemplify his simultaneous interest in abstract as well as naturalistic forms: *Head of the Father* [*flat I*] 1927–30 (p.36) presents a flat face with 'simplified' features, setting it apart from the round form of the head as a whole, while *Head of the Father* [*round II*] c.1927–30 shows Giovanni's face in a more 'realistic' style (p.37).

In a photograph taken by Marc Vaux around 1928 (above), three 'plaque' sculptures of heads are shown together with

'Plaque' sculptures c.1928

the sculpture *Man and Woman* 1928–9 (p.40), emphasising the flatness of the heads by juxtaposing them with the pointed, sharp forms of the latter. The positioning of the sculptures and the photographic viewpoint seem to have been paramount. In one of Giacometti's notebooks there are sketches under a note saying 'atelier fotografiare', which prove how Giacometti planned the photographic composition of his sculptures.[12] Comparable to sculptors Auguste Rodin, Brâncuşi and Pablo Picasso, the young Giacometti was well aware of the power of photography in shaping the perception and interpretation of sculptures.

In 1929, Giacometti signed a one-year contract with art dealer Pierre Loeb, who paid him a monthly salary in return for the right to acquire, or exhibit and sell his work. His sculptures were featured increasingly in group shows, for example in Paris at the exhibition *Un Groupe d'Italiens de Paris* at the Salon de l'escalier, and the Galerie Georges Bernheim, and in Zurich at Galerie Wolfensberger. After terminating his contract with Loeb, Giacometti was then represented by Pierre Colle.

SURREALIST YEARS

Surrealism was the avant-garde of the time. It was the only group of artists where something was happening.[13]

In 1931, surrealist artist Salvador Dalí reacted with excitement to a sculpture by Giacometti, *Suspended Ball* 1930–1 (p.43), that he had seen at Galerie Pierre, where Giacometti's latest works were exhibited in the company of those by Joan Miró and Jean Arp. He wrote: 'a wooden ball, stamped with a feminine groove and hanging from a fine violin string over a crescent, one edge of which barely grazes the cavity. The viewer finds himself instinctively forced to make the ball slide along the edge, but because of the length of the string he is not able to do this properly.'[14] Fighting against tradition, morality and the bourgeoisie, the members of the artistic and literary movement of surrealism claimed that works of art should channel the unconscious and irrational as a means of unlocking the power of the imagination in everyday reality. *Suspended Ball*, which invites the viewer to move the sphere, was seen as the prototype of a surrealist object. In 1932 Giacometti aligned himself with the left-wing surrealist opposition around writer Louis Aragon, before deciding to participate in some activities of the surrealist group led by André Breton. In 1932, Pierre

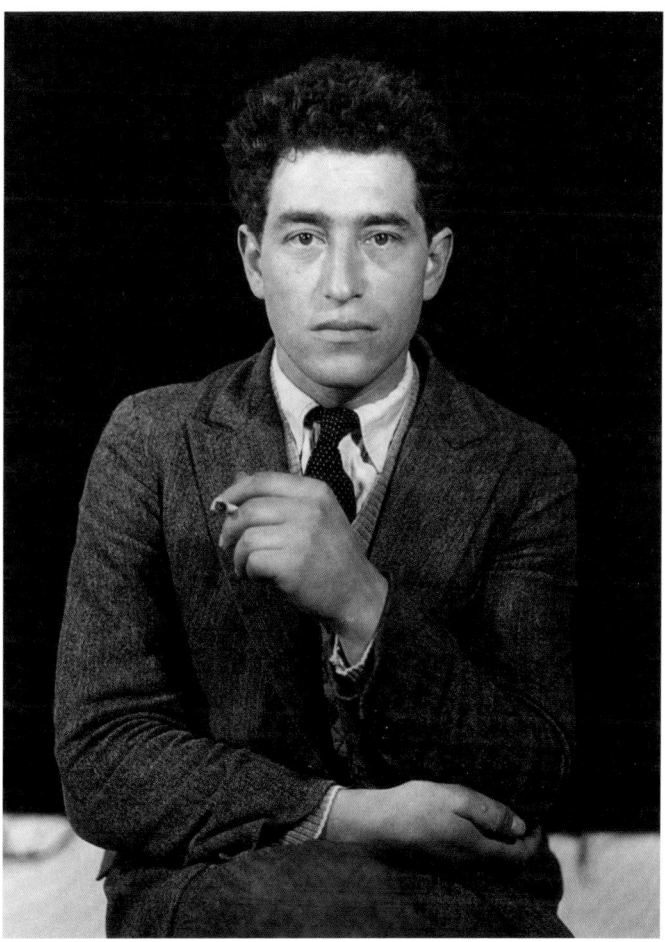

Colle mounted Giacometti's first solo exhibition and Picasso was among the first visitors.

Giacometti created a number of works inspired by surrealism, including *Cage* 1930–1 (p.42), *Disagreeable Object* 1931 in plaster, bronze, and wood (p.46), and *Man, Woman, Child* 1931 (pp.44–5). He published in surrealist journals, exhibited with other surrealist artists at the Salon des surindépendants in 1933 and frequented bars and brothels, such as Le Sphinx in Montparnasse, which was a favourite artists' haunt. The bronze sculpture *Woman with Her Throat Cut* 1932 (pp.48–9), exhibited on a low plinth or directly on the floor, conveys a feeling of violence and brutal sexuality that can be found in

Albrecht Dürer
Melencolia I 1514
Engraving
24 × 18.8

Lunar 1933
Ink on paper
27.5 × 20

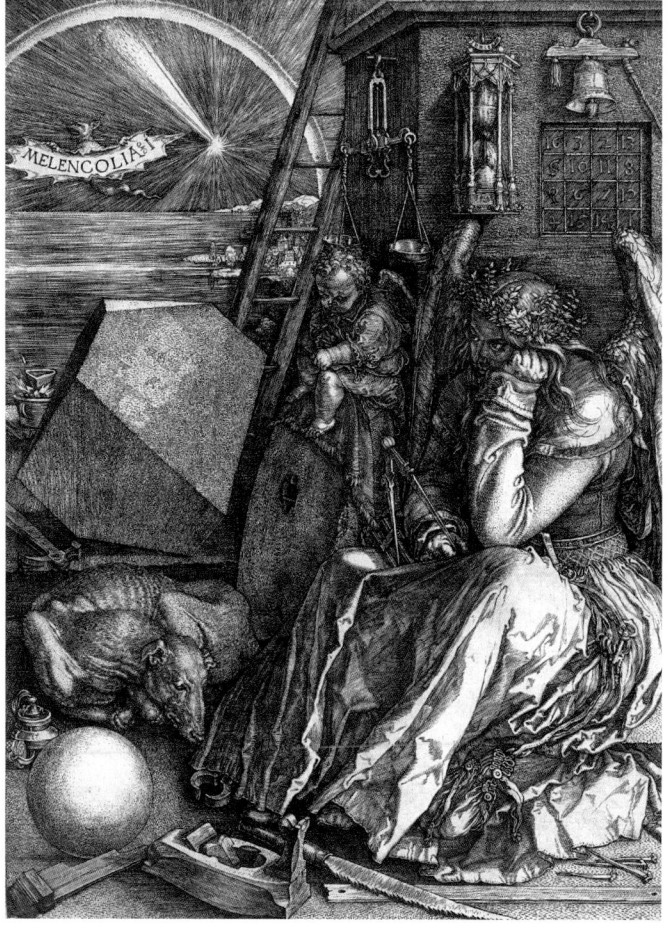

several works from this era: the abstracted insect-like female appears to be disembowelled and in the throes of death, while her tense, pointed forms also suggest a trap that might shut tight if her torso is touched.

Giacometti's most abstract work from his surrealist phase is *Cube* 1933–4 (p.50): a large irregular polyhedron, which exists in plaster as well as bronze and also appears in drawings, such as *Lunar* 1933 (opposite). The closed geometric form conveys an introverted feeling, inspired by Dürer's engraving *Melencolia I* 1514 (above). Interestingly, Giacometti scratched a small face into the underside of the cube, linking the geometric shape to a human head.[15]

After the death of his father, Giacometti remained with his mother for a few months, creating a tombstone for his father's grave at Borgonovo cemetery. Meanwhile, in New York, the Julien Levy Gallery organised Giacometti's first exhibition in the United States.

When Giacometti returned to Paris, he continued his studies of heads, with his brother Diego and professional model Rita Gueyfier sitting for him. For the surrealists around Breton, these 'realistic' works after models constituted treason and Giacometti left the group. However, he remained in contact with some artists, such as Paul Éluard and Max Ernst, and agreed to include his works in surrealist exhibitions. In London in 1936, the New Burlington Galleries presented the *International Surrealist Exhibition*, which was organised by British poets David Gascoyne and Hugh Sykes Davies with Breton, among others. It featured works from Great Britain and Continental Europe, including Giacometti's *Spoon Woman* and *Walking Woman* 1932 (p.47). The *Evening News* criticised the exhibition in a short article entitled 'Surrealist Art is Clumsy as well as Meaningless'. Stating that the works displayed were 'not worth looking at', the article featured a photograph of *Spoon Woman* with the ironic subtitle 'here is a "feminine figure"'.[16] However, the exhibition and accompanying lectures were well attended by the public and members of the art world alike.

DECORATIVE ART

Objects interest me hardly any less than sculpture, and there is a point at which the two touch.[17]

During the 1930s, Giacometti produced decorative objects as a means of earning a living: lamps, vases, jewellery and wall reliefs (opposite). He collaborated with well-known interior designer Jean-Michel Frank and was supported by Diego, who had settled into a dual role as his brother's most important male model and his assistant in the workshop. Diego was to become a designer of his own furniture pieces and sculptures later.

Giacometti's decorative pieces were popular and featured in *Vogue* and *Harper's Bazaar*. The sculptor occupied a privileged position among Frank's collaborators and designed some one hundred models. A letter shows Frank humorously encouraging Giacometti to send him new designs: 'Everyone who comes here or to the studio swoons over your works.

Untitled [Decorative Seagull Object] c.1935–7
48 × 160 × 5.1

Untitled [Drawing for Mural] c.1937
Pencil on paper
21 × 27

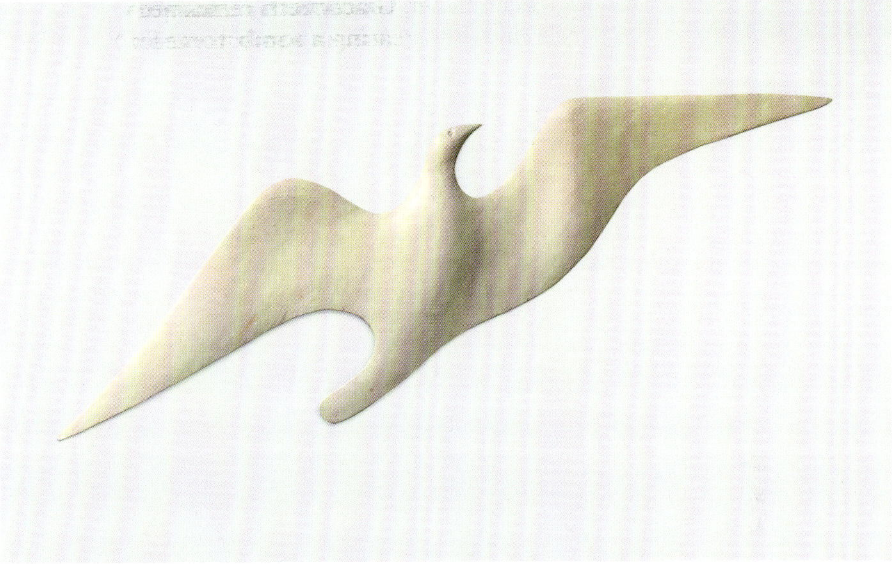

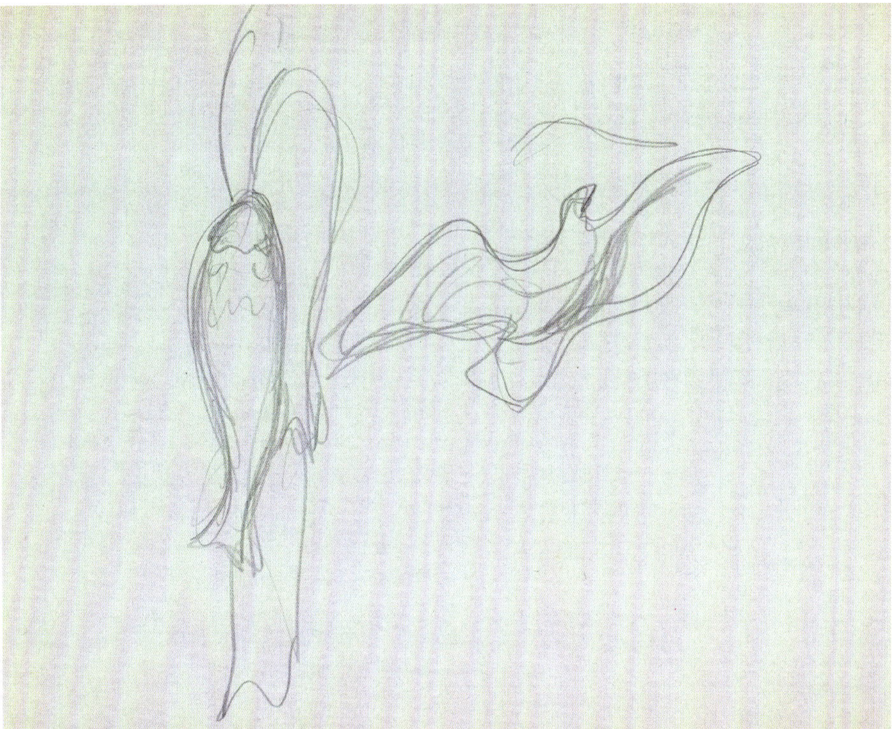

Table 1933
Pen and india ink on paper
22.2 × 18.4

Moving and Mute Objects
Pages 68 and 69 of *Revue* xxe
siècle, no.3, June 1952

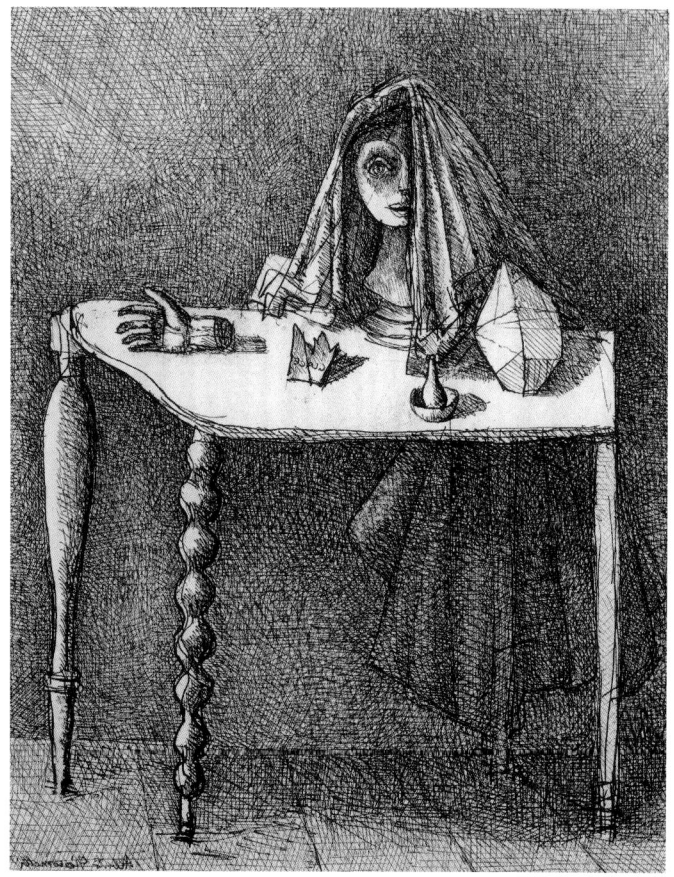

That's the only thing they like. If you make more models, perhaps I'll be able to buy myself a suit. Don't forget me = lamps, vases, and when will there be furniture?'[18] Giacometti did not think of the decorative arts as minor and on several occasions his decorative works influenced his practice as a sculptor, and vice versa. In *Table* 1933 (above, p.51) Giacometti seems to be creating a synthesis of the arts by making a mysterious composite sculpture with decorative elements placed on a table. The work also exemplifies how he often used both sculpture and drawing to illustrate similar motifs in different media. Drawing was not only a means of preparing for sculptures but was also used as an art form in its own right, presenting finished sculptures in atmospheric compositions, as symbols of art.

Heads and figures only seemed true to me when very small.[19]

On 1 September 1939 the Second World War broke out. After the invasion of France by Nazi German forces, Giacometti went to Geneva to visit his mother. His sister Ottilia had died in 1937 after giving birth to her son Silvio, and Giacometti's mother was raising her grandchild. Denied a French re-entry visa, Giacometti spent the rest of the war period in Switzerland, while Diego looked after the studio in Paris. Giacometti continued to focus on sculpture and portrayed Silvio in numerous drawings and figures (p.54). Most sculptures from these years are very small, suggesting the appearance of a person seen from a distance. Giacometti recollected that one evening in Paris, he saw his close friend, the English artist Isabel Nicholas (later Lambert and Rawsthorne), from afar on the Boulevard Saint-Michel. He claimed that this experience led him to attempting to capture a human presence in small size: 'I had a friend, an English girl ... I wanted to make a sculpture of this woman as I had once seen her some distance away on the street – it was very impressive.'[20]

Living and sculpting in a hotel room in Geneva, Giacometti regularly met with friends, including publisher Albert Skira, photographer Eli Lotar and artist Balthus. In 1943 he became

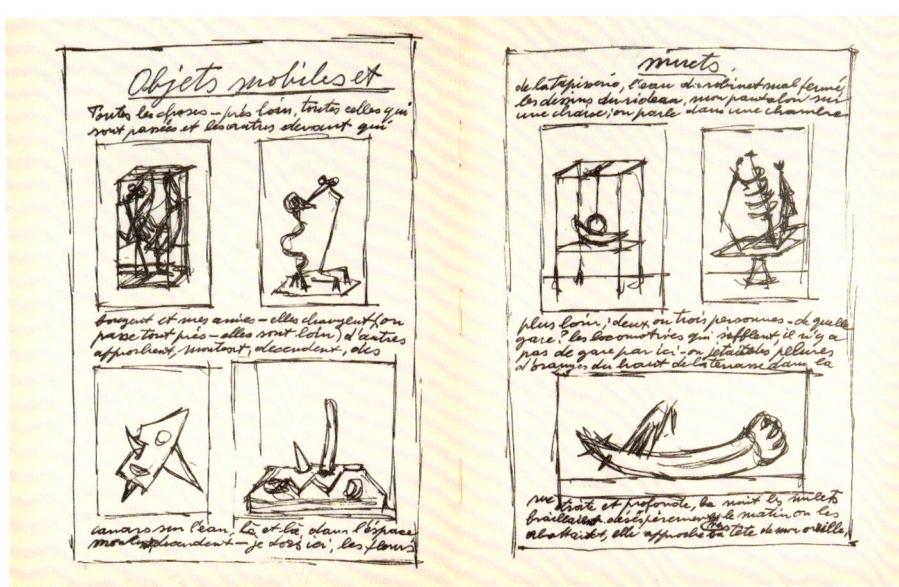

acquainted with Annette Arm, a young woman who worked in an office at the Red Cross. A few years later, she was to become his wife and most important female model.

In Stampa, Giacometti created the only large sculpture of this period, *Woman with Chariot* c.1945, which later inspired him to create his well-known work *The Chariot* 1950 (p.62). In this later work, rising above two high wheels recalling those of an ancient Egyptian carriage, a slender elongated female figure stands in equilibrium, slightly raising her arms. Giacometti claimed that this masterwork was partly inspired by the memory of a pharmacy cart that he had seen when briefly hospitalised.

Giacometti and Isabel wrote to each other during the war. In a long letter from 30 July 1945, more than two months after the war had ended in Europe, Giacometti noted: 'it is my sculptures that hold me back here in Geneva, keeping me now in a suspended life next to it all, making it impossible to return sooner.'[21]

POSTWAR & EXISTENTIALISM

I wanted to hold on to a certain height, and they became narrow ... The more I wanted to make them broader, the narrower they got.[22]

In September 1945, Giacometti returned to Paris with, as legend has it, six matchboxes containing the small sculptures he had made in Geneva. He began to paint again and gradually found his way to the elongated sculptures with rugged surfaces that characterise his postwar works. The large, extremely slender figures, such as *Walking Man* 1947, *Standing Woman* 1948 and *Falling Man* 1950 (p.59), mark the emergence of this mature style. He also started to create a series of compositions with figural groupings in different spatial situations, including *The Square* 1948 (pp.60–1). Other sculptures from the late 1940s, such as *The Nose* and *The Hand* 1947 (p.56), combine the thin human form with a mystical language reminiscent of Giacometti's surrealist phase, often featuring body parts and cage structures. In 1951, Giacometti sculpted a cat and a dog (pp.64–5). The gaunt dog seems to carry all the weight of the world on his back while continuing to move forward slowly. The expressive sculpture, often interpreted as a self-portrait of the artist, has become a popular work, with admirers ranging from writer Jean Genet to actress Marlene Dietrich.

Giacometti's postwar art and life soon became associated with existentialist ideas, both in Europe and the United States.

The catalyst for this was an essay entitled 'The Search for the Absolute' written by Giacometti's friend, philosopher Jean-Paul Sartre, for an exhibition at the Pierre Matisse Gallery in New York in 1948. According to Sartre, Giacometti's figures are intertwined with the distance between and around them, revealing the crucial role of human perception and the gaze of other people. Sartre's preface includes echoes of his existentialist treatise *Being and Nothingness* (1943), interpreting the attenuated forms and alienated figure ensembles as embodying angst and isolation. In proposing that at first sight they might suggest 'the fleshless martyrs of Buchenwald', Sartre linked Giacometti's thin figures to the gruesome history of the war, creating a contemporary relevance.[23] Although he then juxtaposed the first impression with a description of the works as 'fine and slender natures that rise up to heaven' and as 'dances' and 'glorious bodies', the association with the concentration camp bodies has become a prominent interpretation, reflecting a dark postwar zeitgeist. Through extreme reduction, Giacometti succeeded in sculpting a strong image of humanity and vulnerability in which a generation traumatised by the war could recognise itself.

In Paris, Giacometti's postwar works were shown for the first time in 1951, at the Galerie Maeght. The exhibition helped to establish his fame in Europe. In London, in 1953, the Hanover Gallery exhibited his sculptures, including *The Square*, together with works by Giacomo Manzù, Marino Marini and Henry Moore. Art critic and curator David Sylvester described Giacometti's work as a symbol of modern life: 'all the tantalising mystery of a waiting woman, all the secret purposefulness of men walking anonymously towards and past us, are made visible in these twig-like fragments of bronze.'[24] On the initiative of Sylvester, the Institute of Contemporary Arts in London devoted two symposia to Giacometti. In 1955, the first museum exhibition in Germany of Giacometti's work was shown in Krefeld, Düsseldorf and Stuttgart. Two extensive retrospectives were presented simultaneously: one by the Arts Council Gallery in London, the other by the Solomon R. Guggenheim Museum in New York. Giacometti's works began to enter public art collections.

The Tate Gallery, under the directorship of John Rothenstein, acquired its first works by Giacometti in 1949: the sculpture *Man Pointing* 1947 and the painting *Seated Man* 1949.

In France, the Musée de Grenoble purchased Giacometti's sculpture *The Cage* 1949–50 and became the first public French institution to own one of his sculptures. Private collectors, such as American industrialist and banker George David Thompson, now bought his works systematically.

In 1958, Giacometti was commissioned to create sculptures for the new Chase Manhattan Plaza in New York. However, the commission was never completed – unsatisfied by the relationship between the sculptures and the unfamiliar site in New York, Giacometti later abandoned the project.

RETURN TO PAINTING

Sometimes I think that I am going to capture the apparition and then I lose it and must start afresh.[25]

While still sculpting figures drawn from memory, in 1946 Giacometti returned to working from the model in painting. After Annette moved into his studio in Paris, she became his most important female model, enduring long portraiture sittings. Giacometti painted her as an entire figure (opposite) or close up, and on occasion nude. The portraits show her face-on, perhaps to reflect her frank and straightforward character.

Most portrait paintings by Giacometti depict the people who inhabited his life: Annette, Diego (p.66), his mother

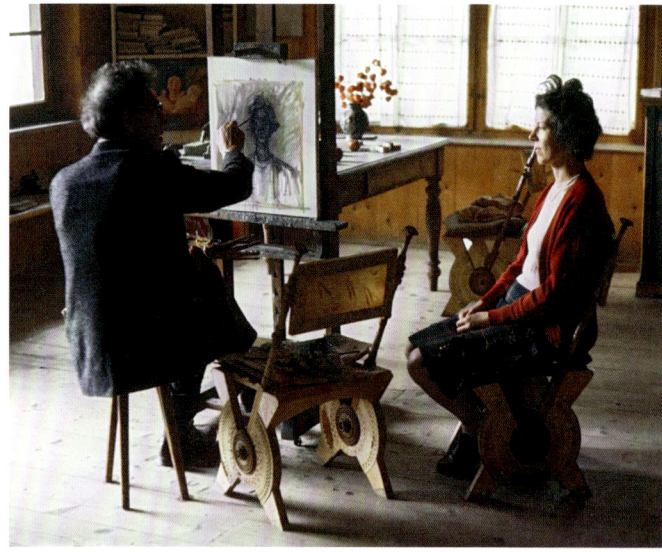

Alberto Giacometti working on a portrait of his wife Annette in the studio in Stampa, around 1965

Annette in the Studio 1961
Oil paint on canvas
146 × 97

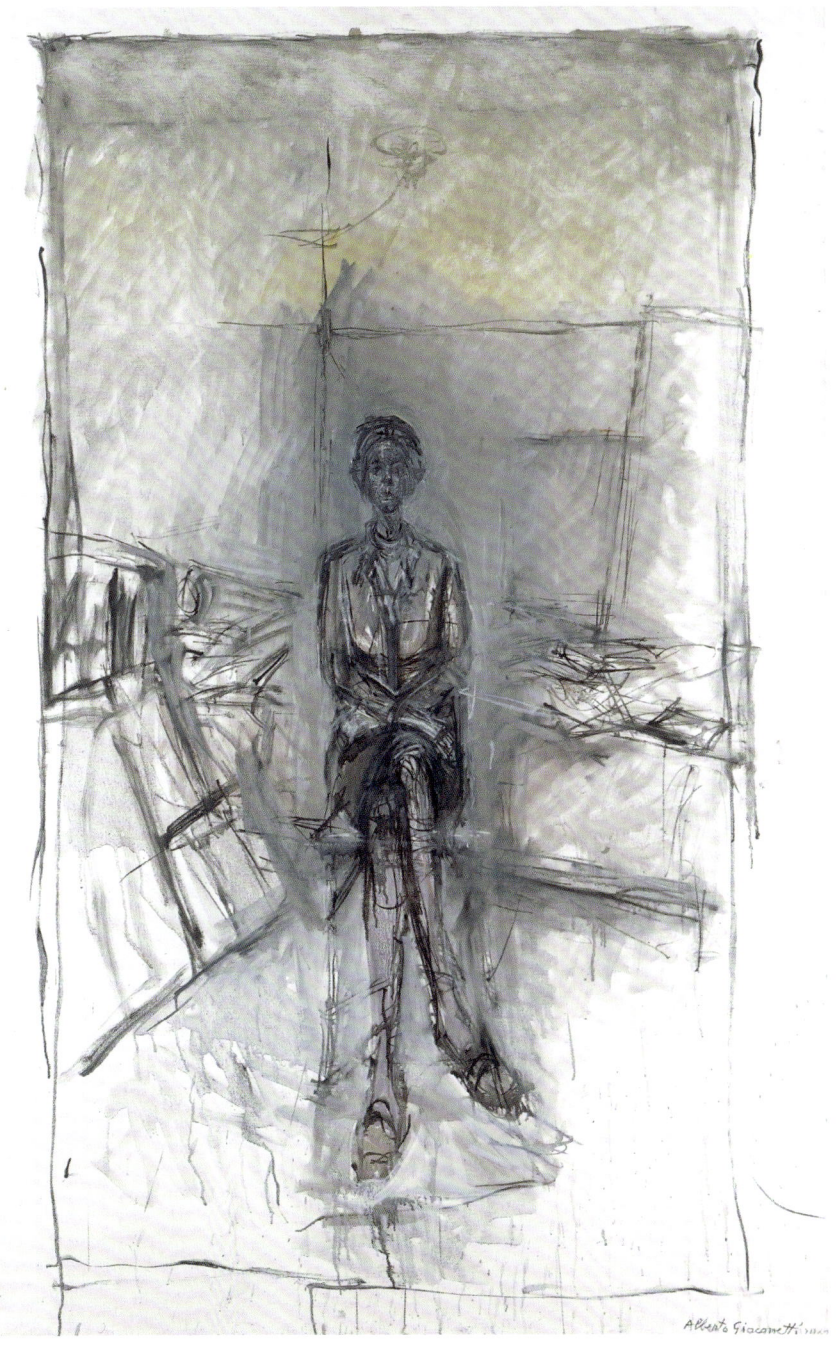

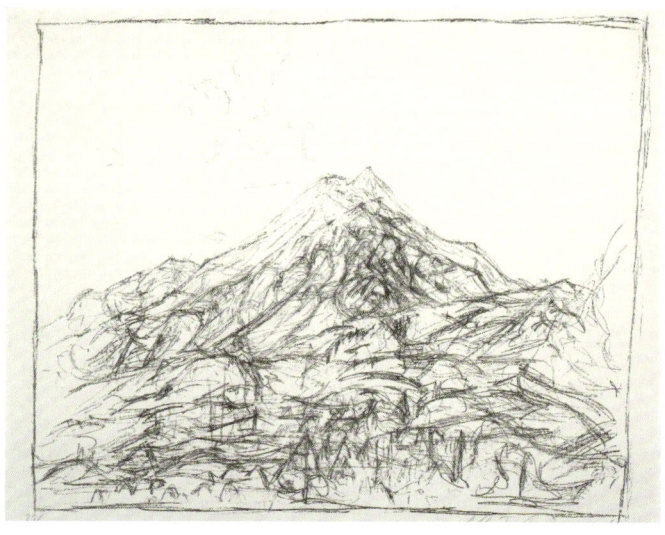

(p.67) and, later, his mistress Caroline (p.75). Giacometti focused on the eyes of his sitter, tracing their movements with the pencil or paintbrush, continuously sketching around the facial forms and dissolving their outlines, while seeking to translate the perceived reality of the human into the reality of the art image. The paintings capture the presence of the portrayed in a flurry of brushstrokes and superimposed washes of paint, resulting in intense, often dark compositions.

In 1954, Giacometti met the writer Jean Genet, who sat for him (p.68) and published recollections of their encounters in his book, *The Studio of Alberto Giacometti*, three years later.

A major subject of Giacometti's paintings is the Japanese professor of philosophy Isaku Yanaihara, who visited Giacometti frequently from 1955 onwards. A friendship developed and he sat for several paintings (p.69). However, Giacometti was not satisfied with the portraits and suffered an artistic crisis, claiming that the works were lacking in likeness. Yanaihara kept journals recording their conversations, which became the basis of a Japanese monograph in 1969.

Giacometti also portrayed his sitters in sculpture, creating numerous busts of Annette (pp.55, 73–4), Diego (p.70) and Yanaihara in plaster and bronze, all conveying an intense human presence. He redeveloped his interest in nature, and made paintings and lithographs of the landscape around Stampa (above), stating that he could spend every day looking at 'the same garden, the same trees, and the same backdrop'.[26] In 1958, he started working on a series of lithographs with views of his Paris milieu, his studio and the surrounding streets and cafés. It was to appear posthumously under the title *Paris sans fin*.

WOMEN OF VENICE

I see my sculptures before me: each one a failure. Yes, I mean it, a failure! But in each one there is also something of what I want to create one day.[27]

In 1956, Giacometti represented France at the 28th Venice Art Biennale. He created a seminal group of sculptures: *Women of Venice* 1956 (p.63). The majestic, elongated nudes, more than one metre in height, reflect Giacometti's lifelong search for an ultimate reality of the female form. At the Biennale, a selection of figures was exhibited alongside works from earlier in his career. After the opening, Giacometti travelled to Bern, where the Kunsthalle was showing a retrospective of his work, also featuring *Women of Venice* plasters (below).

Nine plasters were selected for casting in bronze and exhibited together for the first time at the Pierre Matisse Gallery in New York in 1958. Today, the figures are dispersed internationally: the Tate Gallery acquired the bronze *Woman of Venice* IX in 1959.

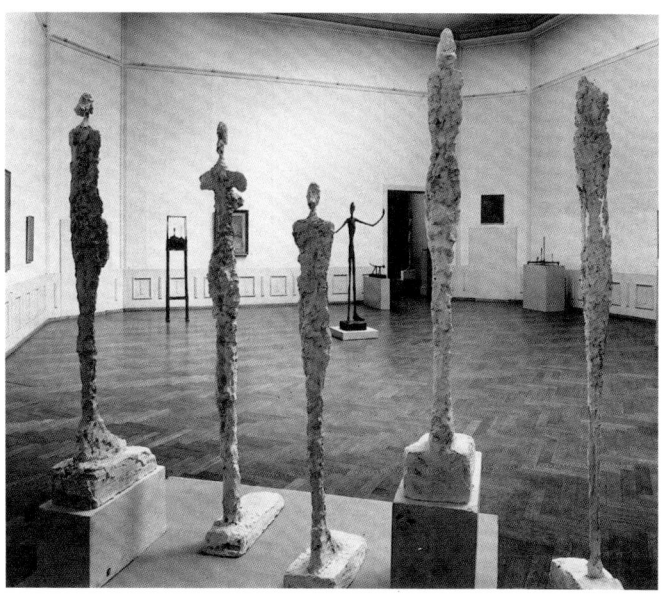

Genet was fascinated by Giacometti's standing female figures: 'For once again I am come back to these women, now in bronze ... I cannot stop myself coming back to this people of gilded – and sometimes painted – sentinels who, upright, immobile, are keeping watch.'[28]

ALBERTO GIACOMETTI: AN ARTISTIC PERSONA

Photograph me like this, Brassaï ... this pose exactly reflects my physical state. I'm nothing but a wreck, a rag ... in spite of that, however, I'm still working, as you can see.[29]

When thinking about Giacometti, the first images that come to mind are the black-and-white photographs taken by professional photographers, particularly from the late 1940s onwards until his death, for example by Ernst Scheidegger (opposite). Giacometti has a gaunt face and wild hair and is surrounded by thin, rugged sculptures in a crammed studio in Paris. He is captured in his own realm, a solitary world of dust and despair, endlessly struggling with unachievable artistic ideals. The photographs of Giacometti in his studio or local cafés have been reproduced in countless books, journals and exhibition catalogues and played an influential role in shaping the artist's public persona.

Since Sartre's text, 'The Search for the Absolute', Giacometti has often been viewed as a serious solo figure, representing a postwar zeitgeist of existentialism and agony. Giacometti, in part, encouraged this image, not only through his written and recorded statements about failure, obsession and fear of death, but also through his 'performances' for the photographic lens. In his book *The Artists of My Life*, photographer and friend Brassaï described an encounter with Giacometti in 1965 in which the artist asked him to photograph him in a particular pose: 'In his weakened condition, he could barely stand upright. He held on to his easel with both hands. "Photograph me like this, Brassaï ... this pose exactly reflects my physical state."'[30] Such recollections by photographers and Giacometti's posing in the images prove how he constructed his artistic persona. Sculpting, drawing and painting from models, he was familiar with the processes of transforming living subjects into objects of art. He knew that photographers would turn him into an object of their works of art too and reacted by perfecting his facial expressions and gestures for the camera. American writer James Lord met Giacometti in the Café des

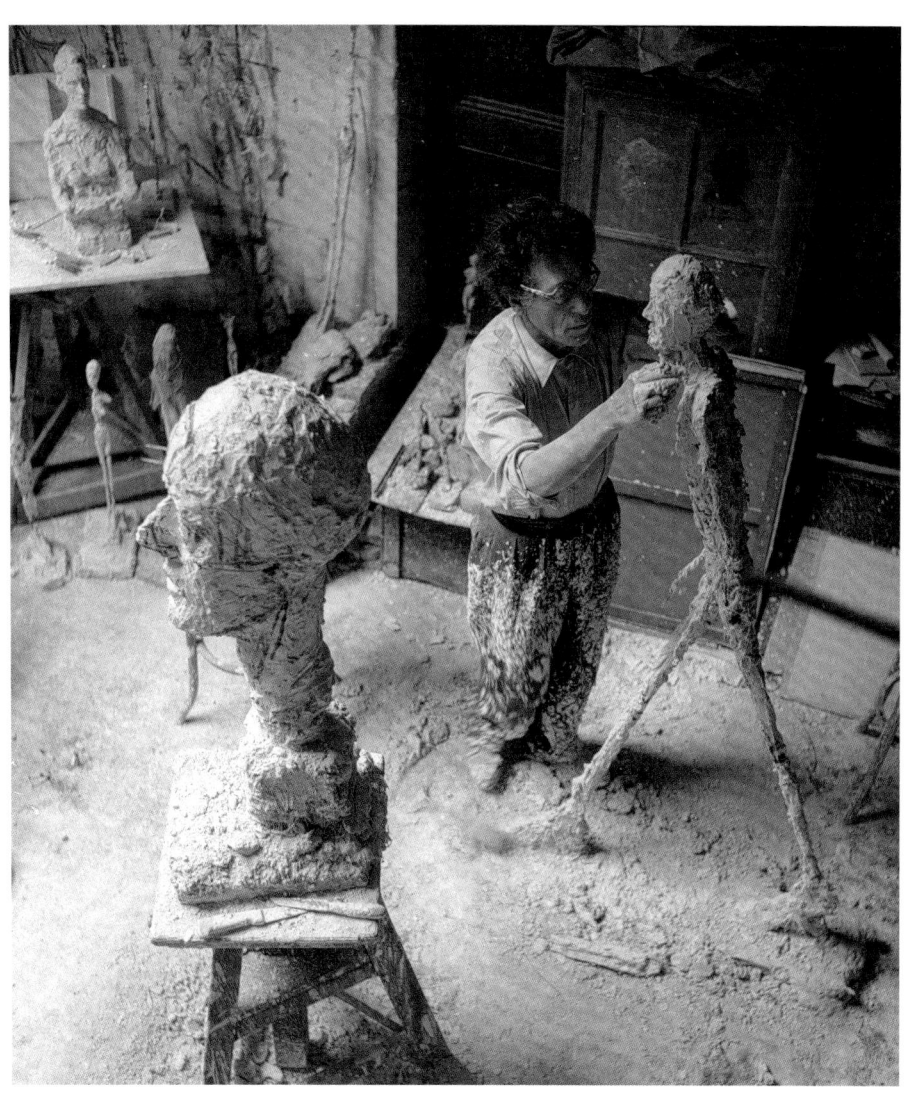

Deux Magots in 1952. Lord's visits to the artist's studio, and conversations with Diego and Giacometti's friends, gave him an intimate knowledge of Giacometti's work and life. He began to collect material for a rather controversial biography that was published in 1985, as well as for the later, and more accurate, *A Giacometti Portrait*, and strengthened the image of Giacometti as a bohemian artist constantly struggling with his unachievable artistic ideals.

Giacometti sculpting his *Walking Man* in plaster c.1962

I began with sculpture because it was the domain that I understood the least. I had to conquer it first to be able to do something else … But I still don't know anything yet, so I have to continue. I don't have a choice.[31]

Giacometti was now a world-famous and well-paid artist. However, his own needs and habits did not change until the end of his days. He wore simple plaster-spattered clothes and worked late into the night. After waking up around noon, his first and only meal before midnight was taken at a café nearby. At night he had a table reserved at the restaurant La Coupole. He continued to go to bars and nightclubs in Saint-Germain-des-Prés and Montparnassse.

An important subject of his late paintings is Caroline. She attracted the much older man's attention when their paths crossed at Chez Adrien, a nightclub frequented by prostitutes, although she claimed not to be one herself. Between 1960 and 1965 Giacometti painted numerous portraits of his mistress, such as *Caroline* 1965 (p.75): 'She sits for me almost every evening from nine to midnight or one o'clock. In the past few years, there haven't been more than four of five evenings that we haven't worked.'[32]

In 1961, Irish writer Samuel Beckett invited Giacometti to design the set for Jean-Louis Barrault's production of his play *Waiting for Godot* at the Théâtre de l'Odéon in Paris. Giacometti created a barren plaster tree and described the process: 'We spent the whole night in the studio with a plaster tree, trying to make it look sparser, smaller, the branches thinner. It never looked any good and neither he [Beckett] nor I liked it. And we kept saying to each other: perhaps like this.'[33]

Giacometti's work was exhibited widely. At the 31st Venice Art Biennale in 1962, he was given his own exhibition area (p.4) and was awarded the Grand Prize for Sculpture, which brought worldwide fame. At the end of the year, he went to the opening of a retrospective at the Kunsthaus Zürich, arranged by his brother Bruno and the museum's director René Wehrli. The Museum of Modern Art, New York, launched a comprehensive travelling exhibition in 1965, while the Tate Gallery, London, organised the retrospective *Alberto Giacometti: Sculpture, Paintings, Drawings 1913–1965*, curated by David Sylvester in consultation with Giacometti. The artist attended both exhibitions.

The Tate Gallery acquired a number of sculptures and two paintings by Giacometti. In a letter to museum director

Giacometti in 1963
in Stampa

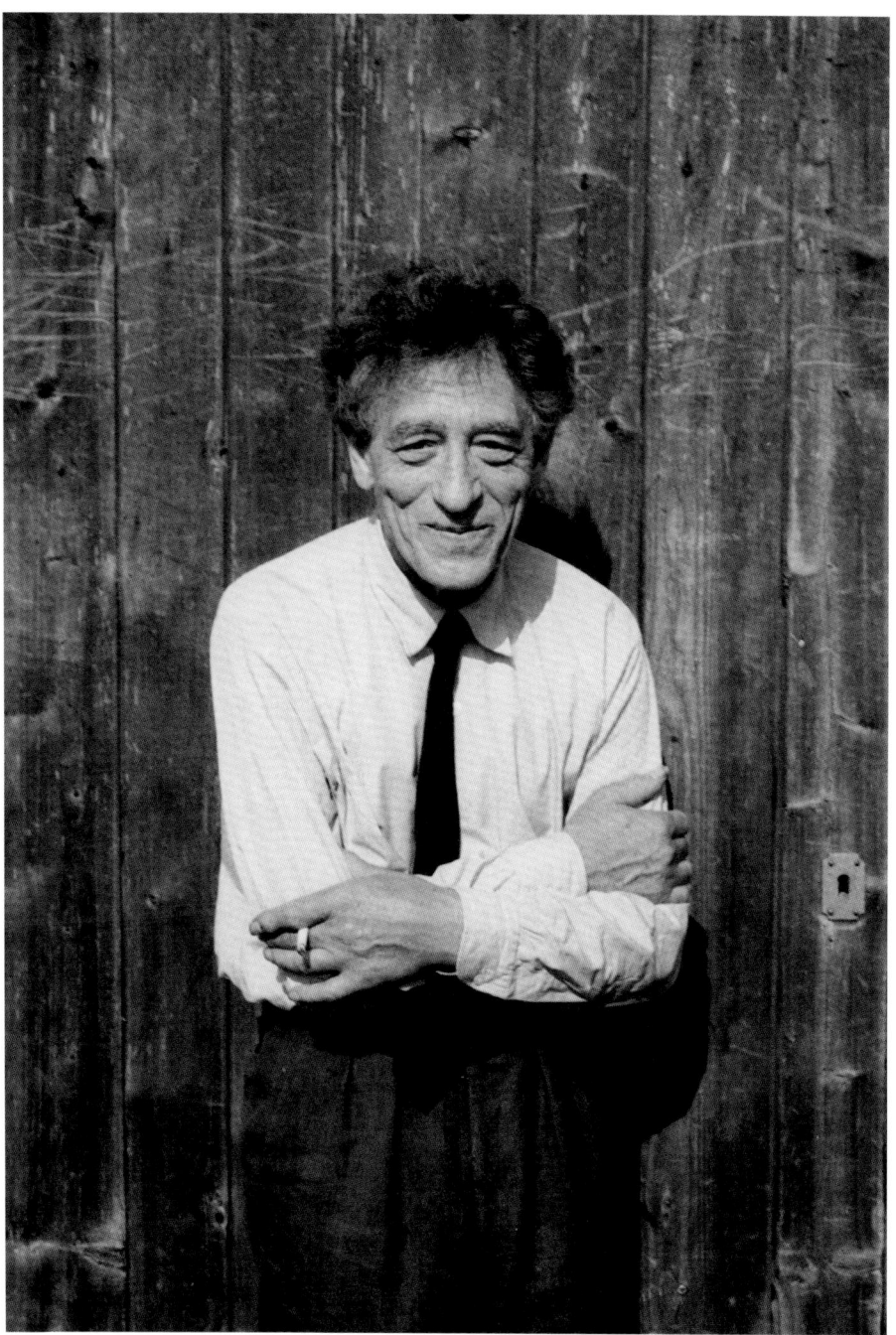

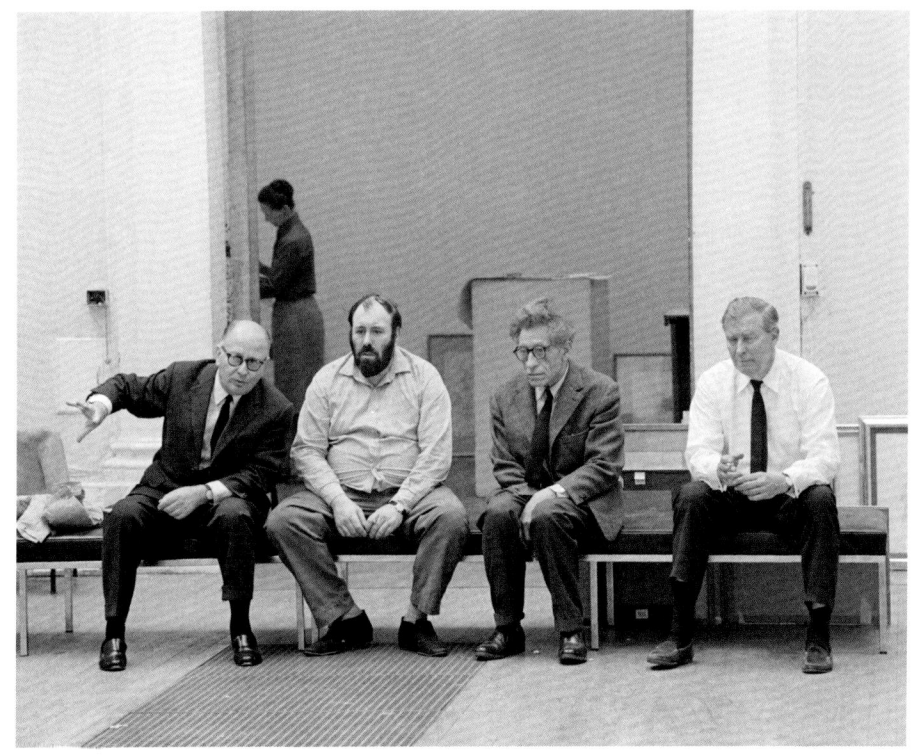

Norman Reid, Giacometti wrote: 'May I tell you again how much I enjoyed my visits to London and how touched I was by your kind welcome ... also how touched and grateful I am that you have chosen so many works for the Tate Gallery. I hope to come to London next spring.'[34] Giacometti was also awarded the Grand Prix National des Arts in France, and an honorary doctorate by Bern University in Switzerland.

In 1963, an ulcer developed into a malignant tumour and large parts of Giacometti's stomach had to be removed. However, he not only resumed his work but also his lifestyle, including working at night and chain-smoking. Brassaï remembered the late Giacometti: 'At the Café-Tabac, Alberto, who was ravenous, downed a sandwich and some hard-boiled eggs that were set out on the bar. He lit one cigarette after another. I was upset to see that he wasn't taking better care of himself.'[35]

In 1964, Giacometti's mother died in Stampa. While Giacometti's tumour was in remission, the artist suffered from

Alberto Giacometti at the Tate Gallery, London, July 1965. Left to right: Louis Clayeux (friend), David Sylvester (organiser), Giacometti and Robin Campbell

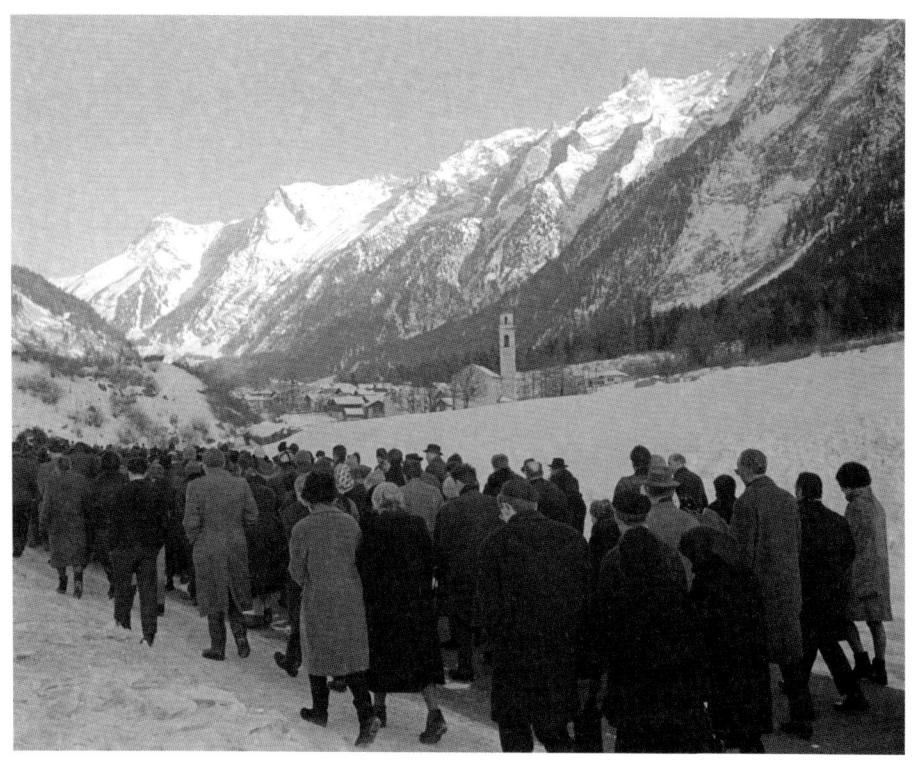

exhaustion. In December 1965, he was hospitalised in Chur, Switzerland, where Annette joined him. When his condition worsened, Diego, Bruno and his wife Odette, and Caroline came to visit. According to his wife, Giacometti said that his work had been 'successful', the opposite of his life, which had 'not been successful'.[36] On 11 January 1966, he succumbed to pericarditis aggravated by years of chronic bronchitis. Four days later, his coffin was taken to the cemetery in Borgonovo. His relatives, people of the Bregaglia valley, Swiss representatives, museum directors and artists paid him their last respects.

Today, Giacometti's works of art feel as strong as ever. They are exhibited worldwide and can be found in many private and public collections. The Alberto Giacometti Foundation, established in Zurich in 1965, regularly displays major works by Giacometti at the Kunsthaus Zürich. In 2003, Annette's bequest led to the establishment of the Fondation Giacometti, Paris, which holds the world's largest collection of Giacometti's works and archival material.

Giacometti's funeral procession to San Giorgio cemetery on 15 January 1966

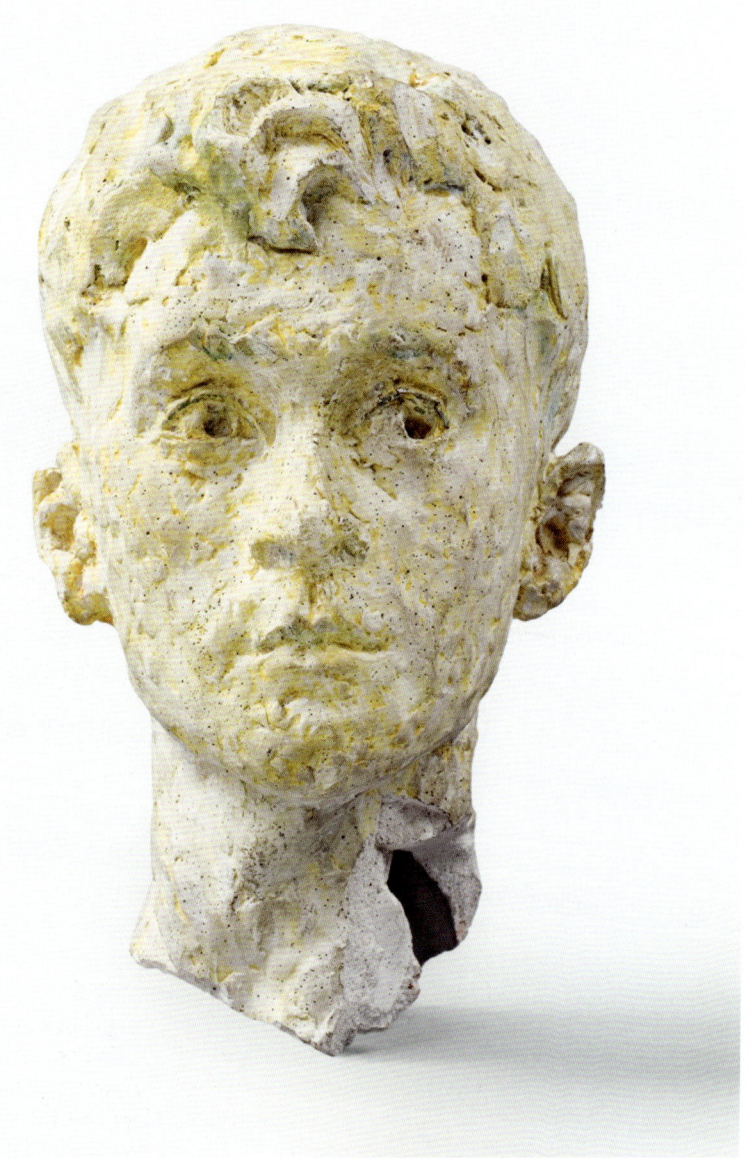

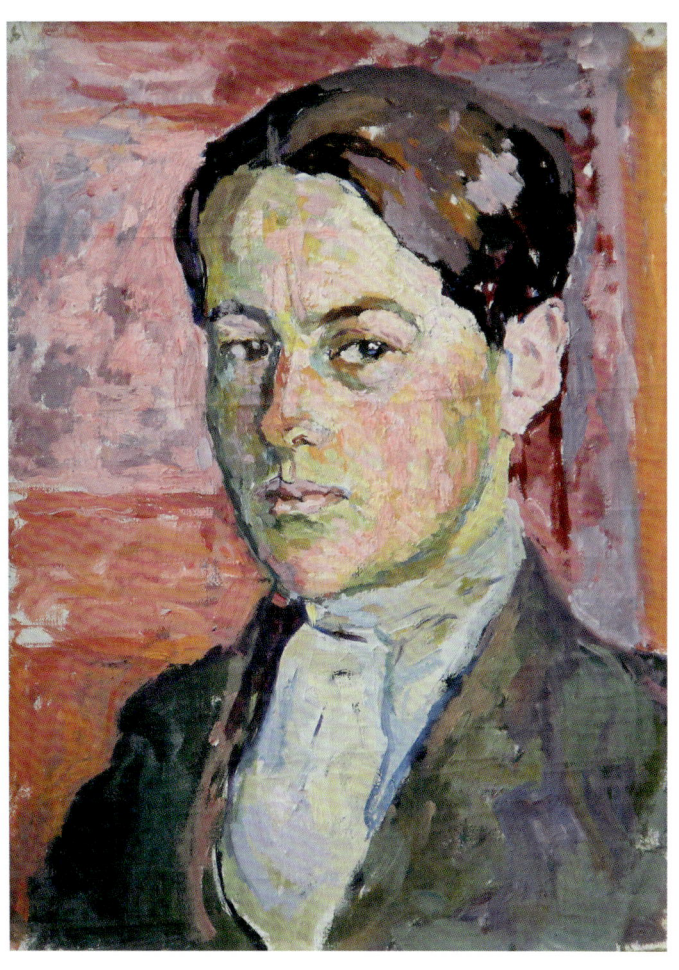

Head of a Child [Simon Bérard]
1917
Painted plaster
22.7 × 12.6 × 16.4

Diego c.1920
Oil paint on canvas
36.4 × 28.3

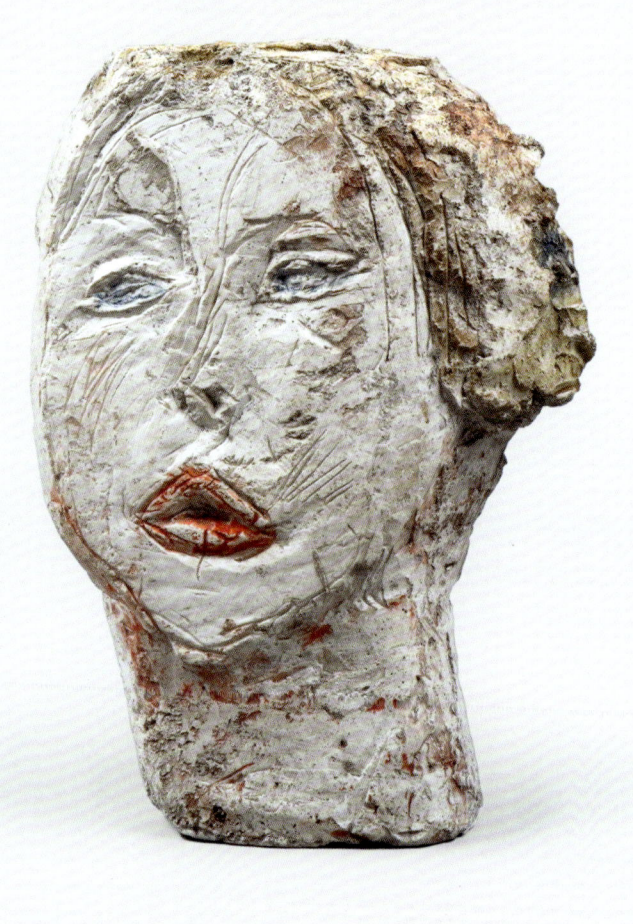

Head of a Woman [Flora Mayo] 1926
Painted plaster
31.2 × 23.2 × 8.4

Cubist Figure I c.1926
Plaster
63.5 × 27.9 × 25.5

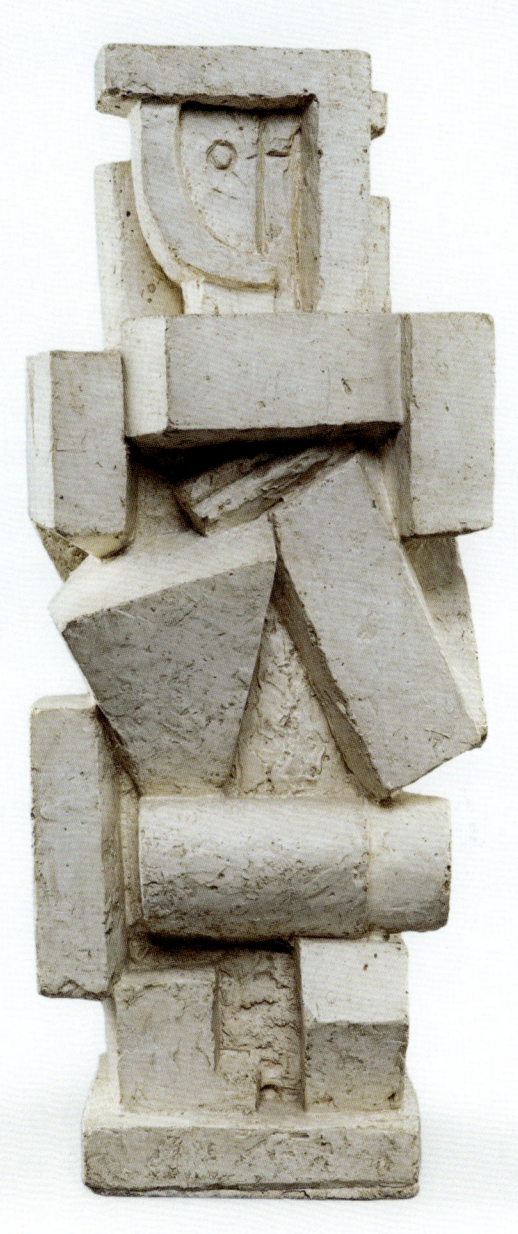

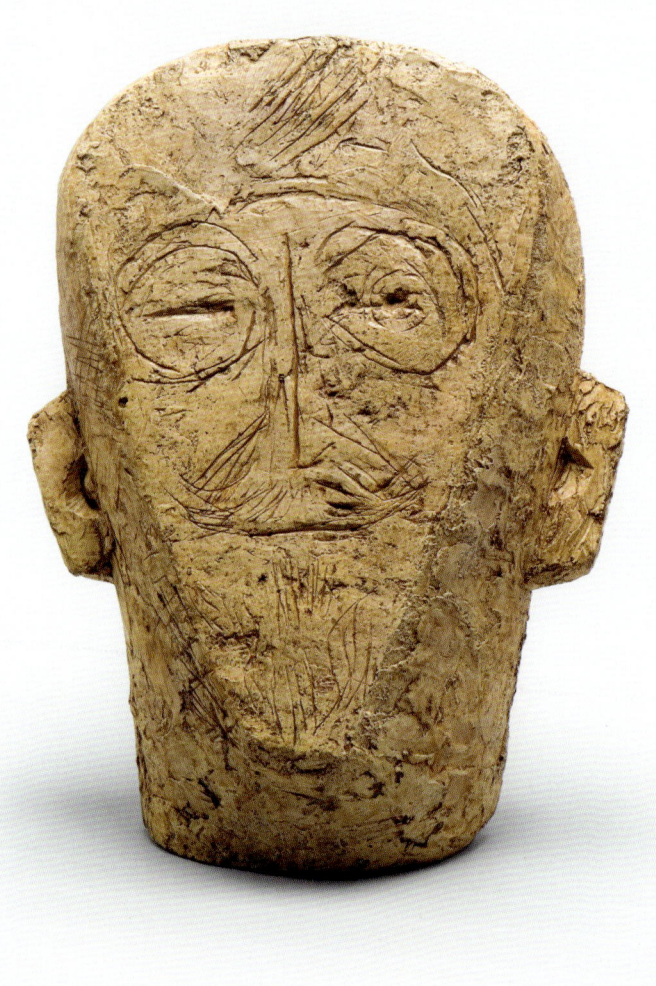

Head of the Father [flat 1]
1927–30
Plaster
28.4 × 22 × 14.6

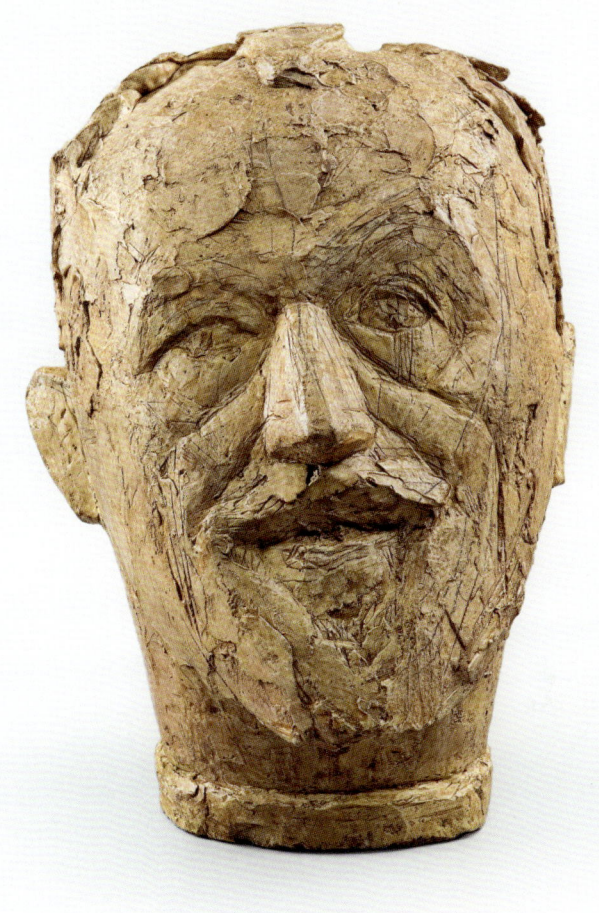

Head of the Father [round II]
c.1927–30
Plaster
28.9 × 21.2 × 23

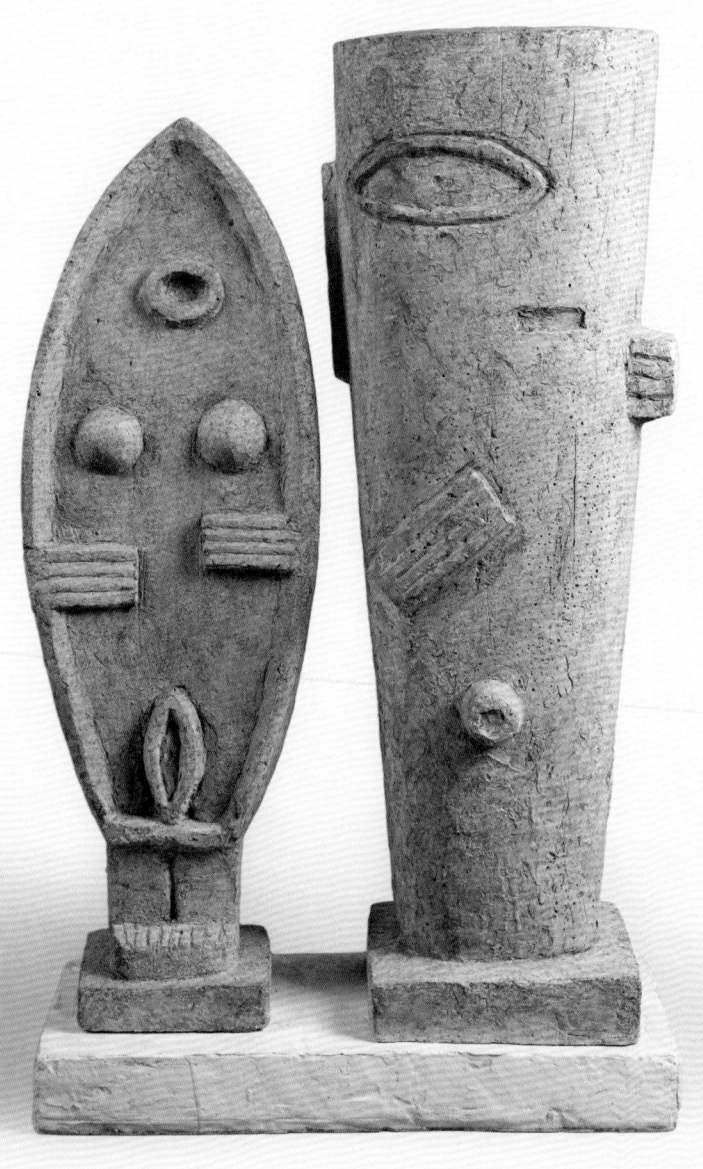

The Couple 1927
Plaster
60.4 × 37.7 × 18

Spoon Woman 1927
Plaster
146.5 × 51.6 × 21.5

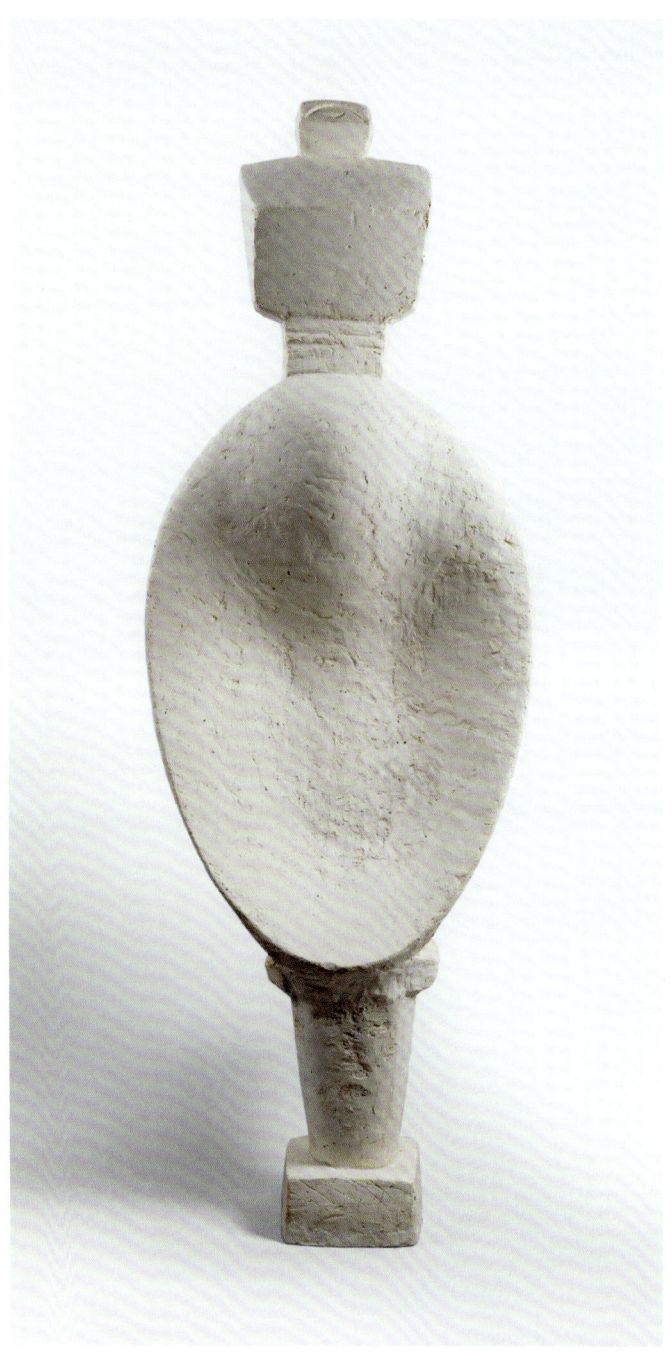

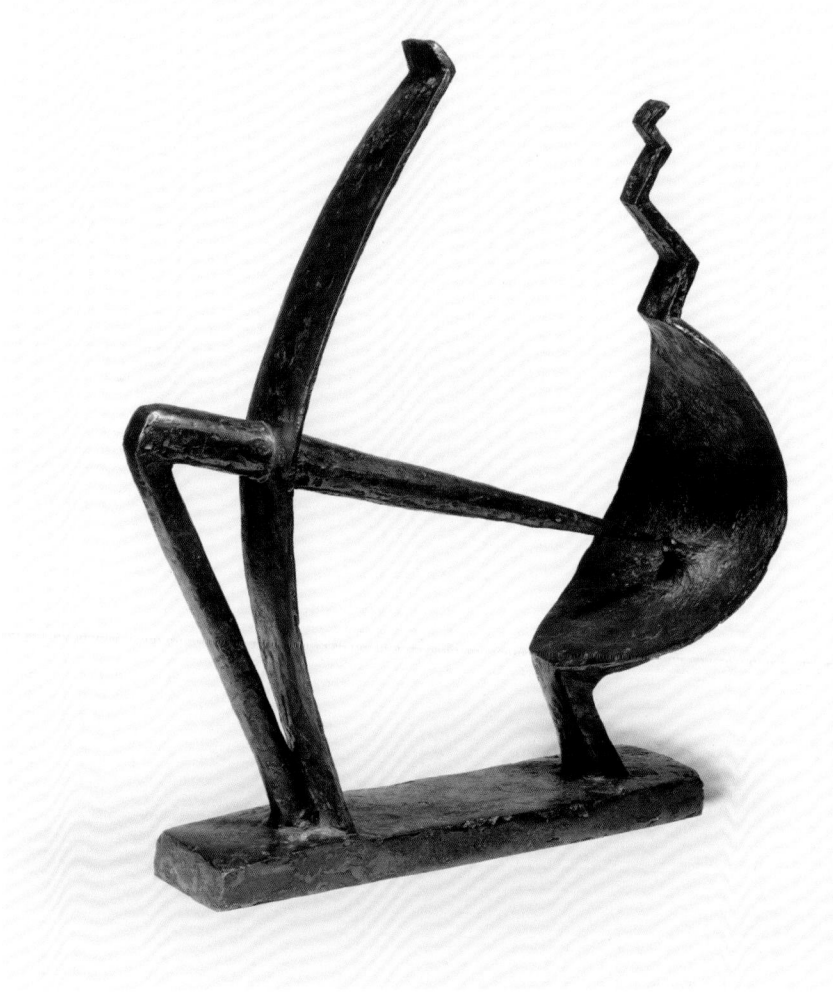

Man and Woman 1928–9
Bronze
40 × 40 × 16.5

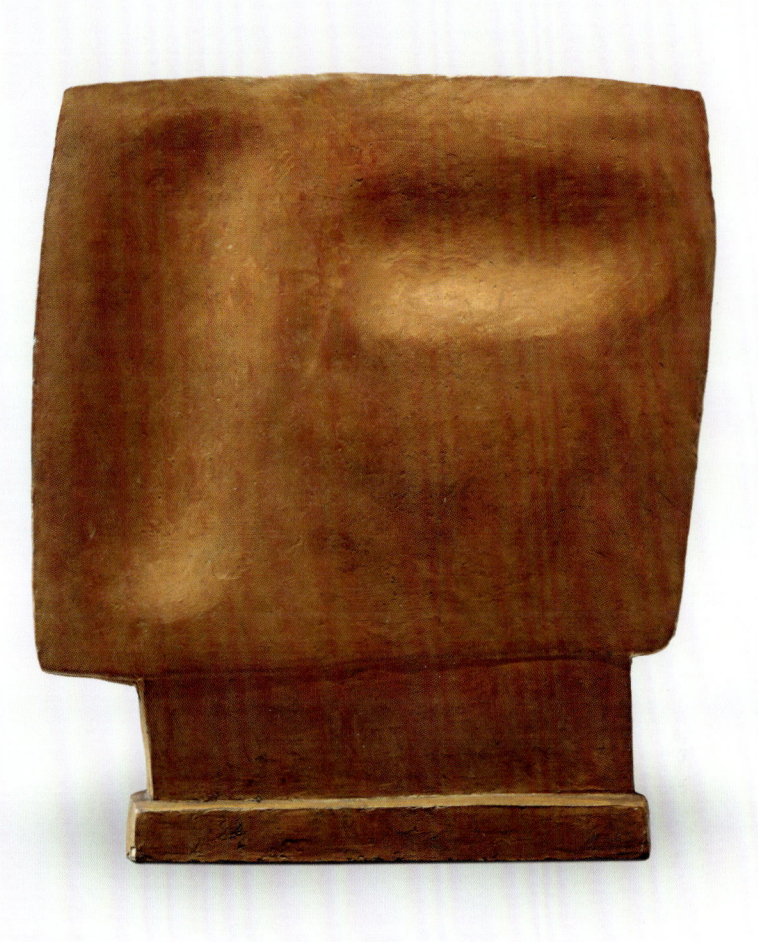

Gazing Head 1929
Terracotta
37 × 33 × 6

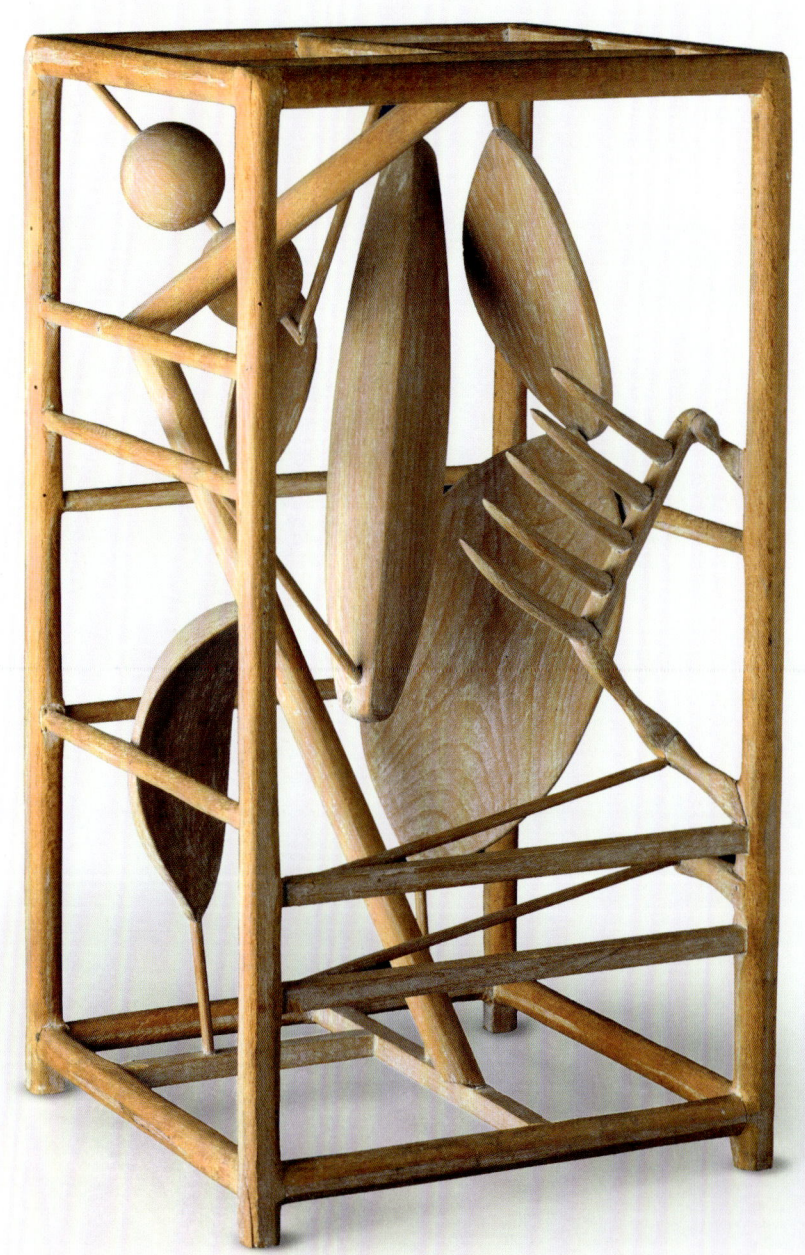

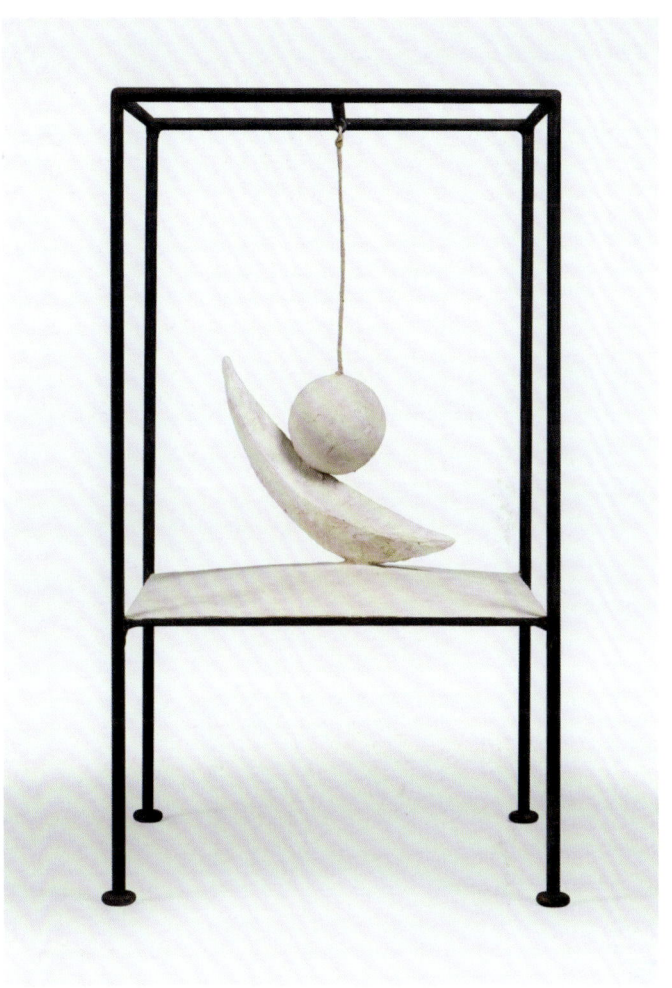

Cage 1930–1
Wood
49.8 × 27 × 27

Suspended Ball 1930–1
Plaster and metal
60.6 × 35.6 × 36.1

OVERLEAF
Man, Woman, Child 1931
Wood and metal
41.5 × 37 × 16

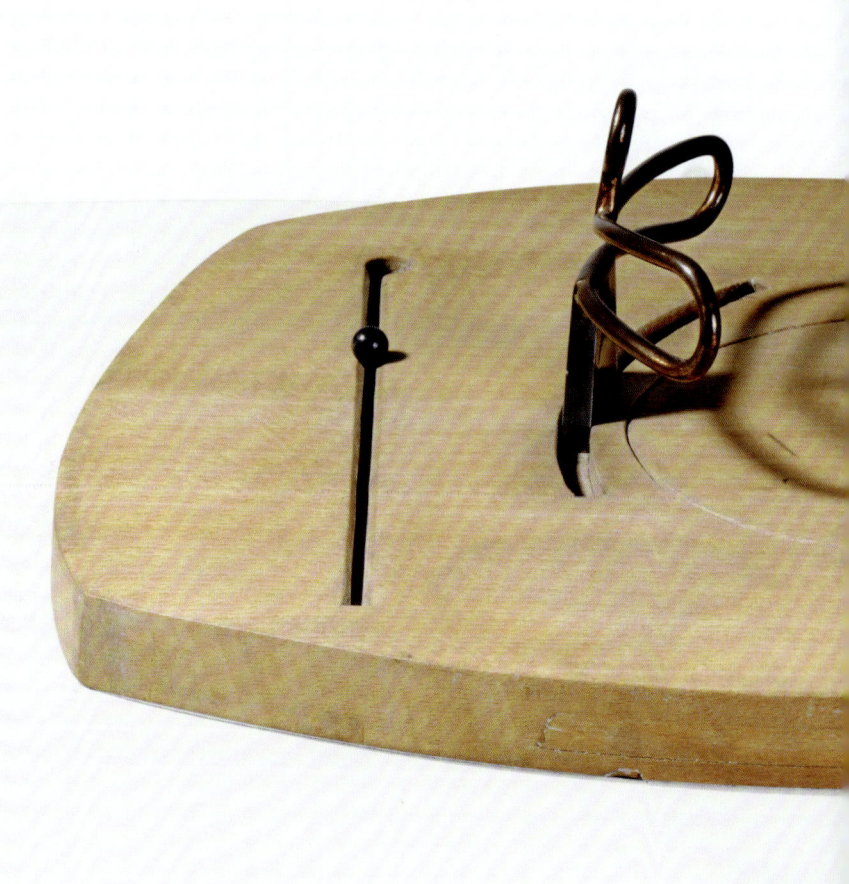

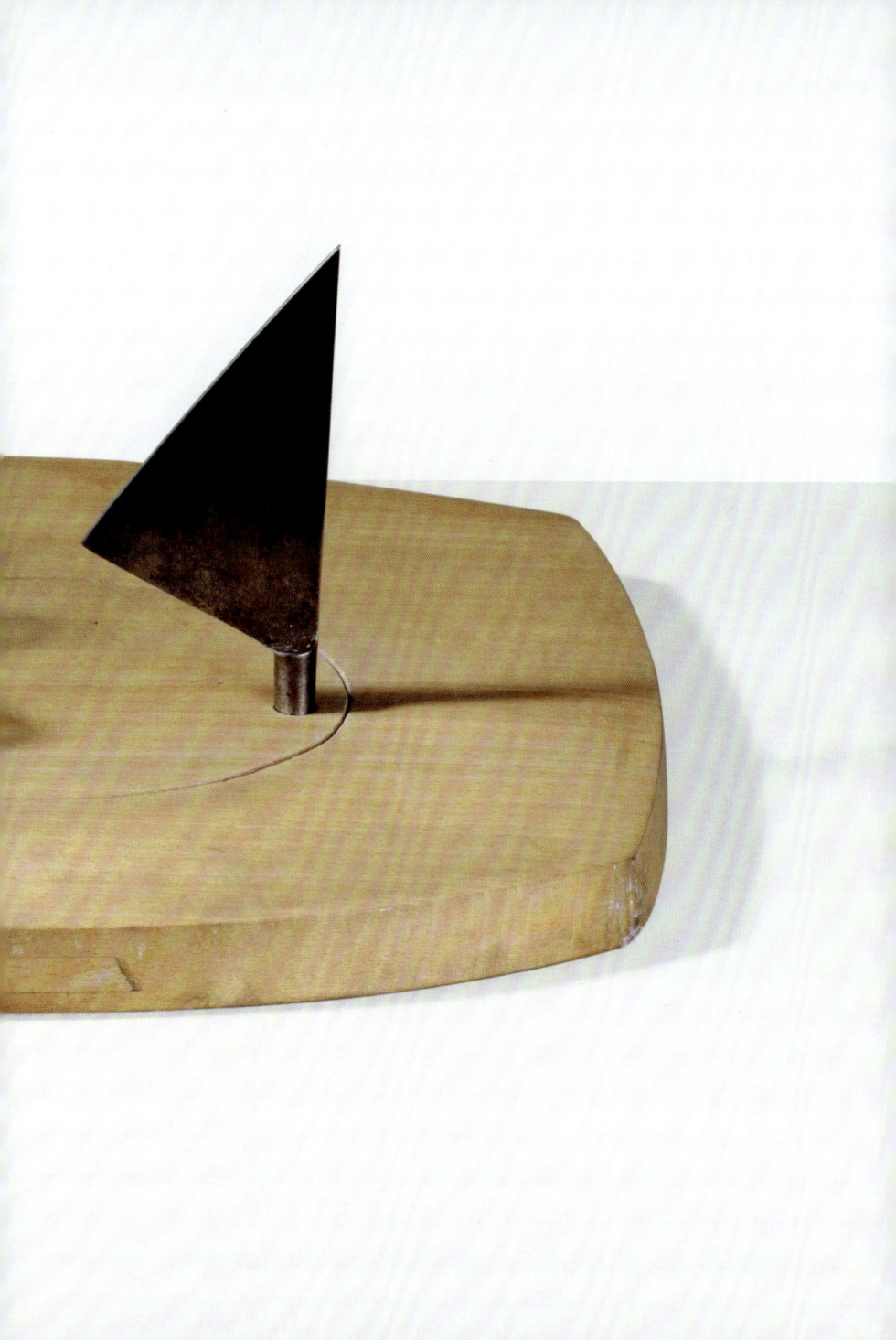

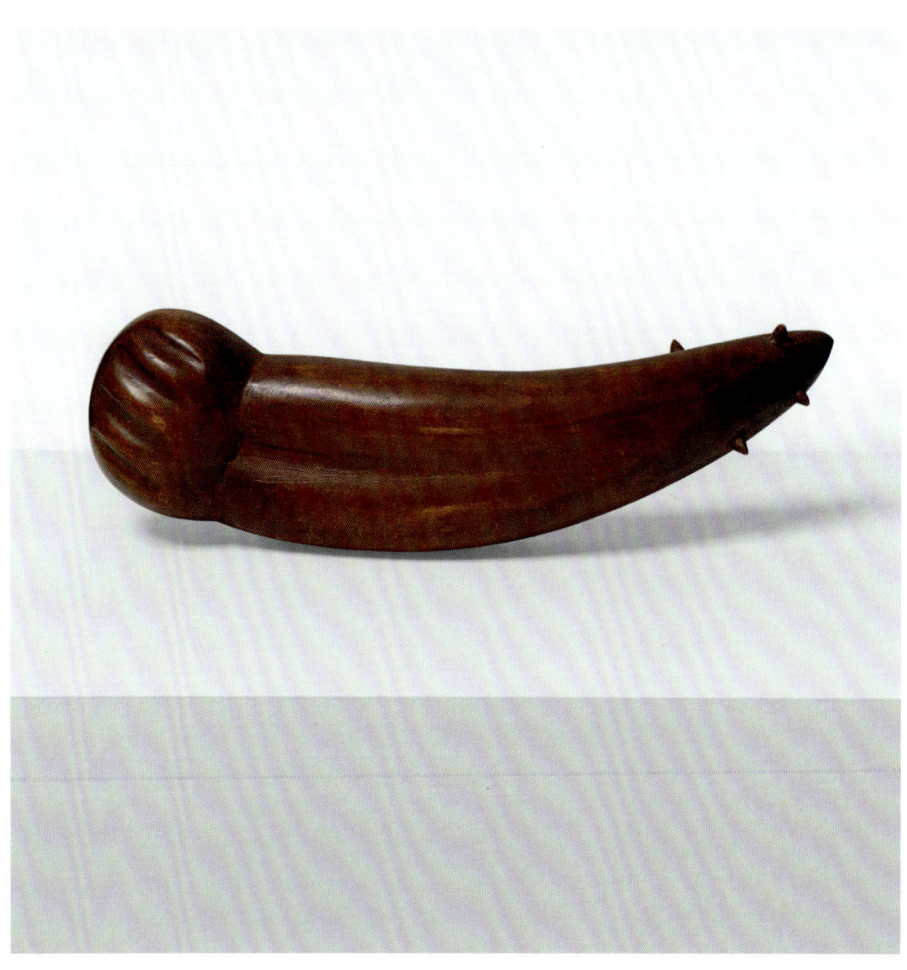

Disagreeable Object 1931
Wood
15.1 × 47.9 × 11.8

Walking Woman 1932
Bronze
149.9 × 27.6 × 37.8

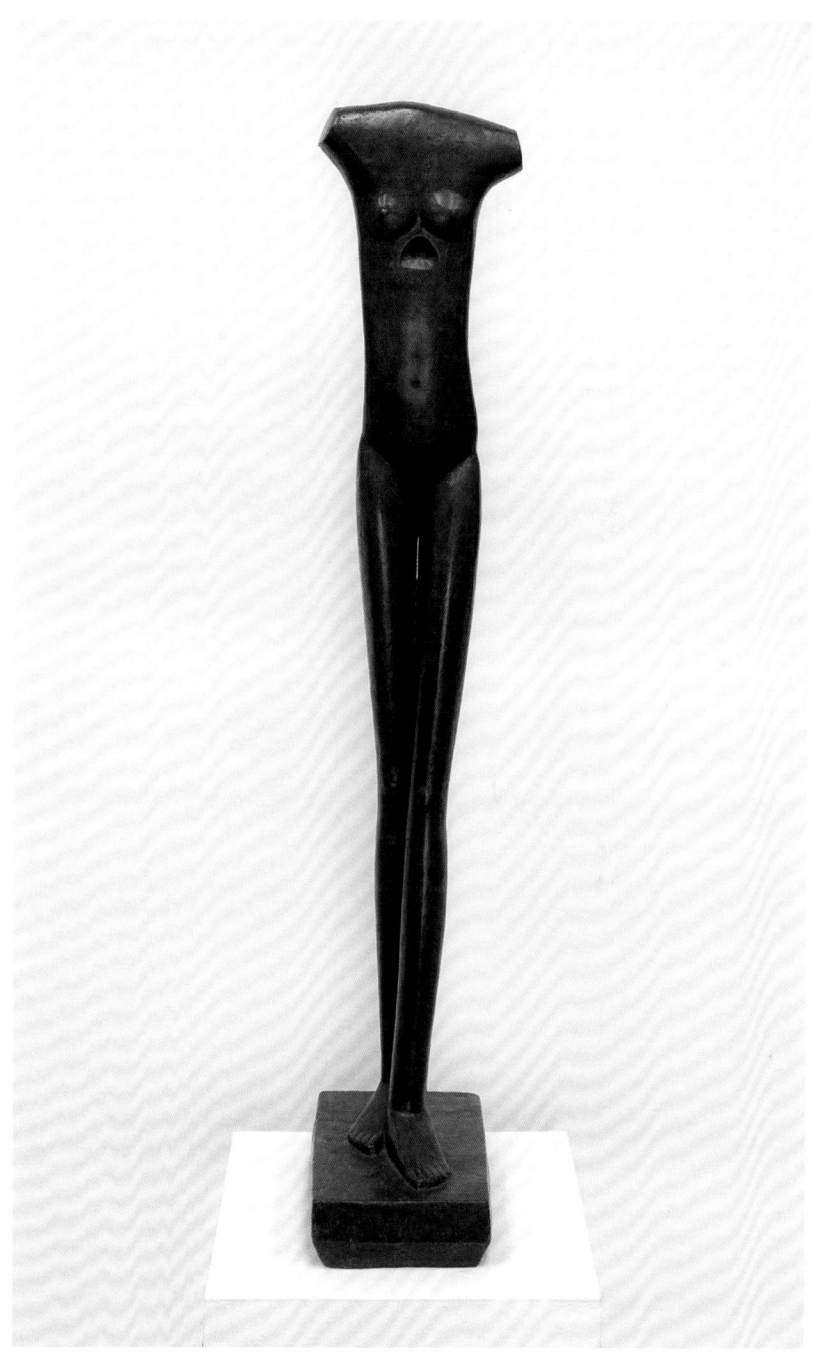

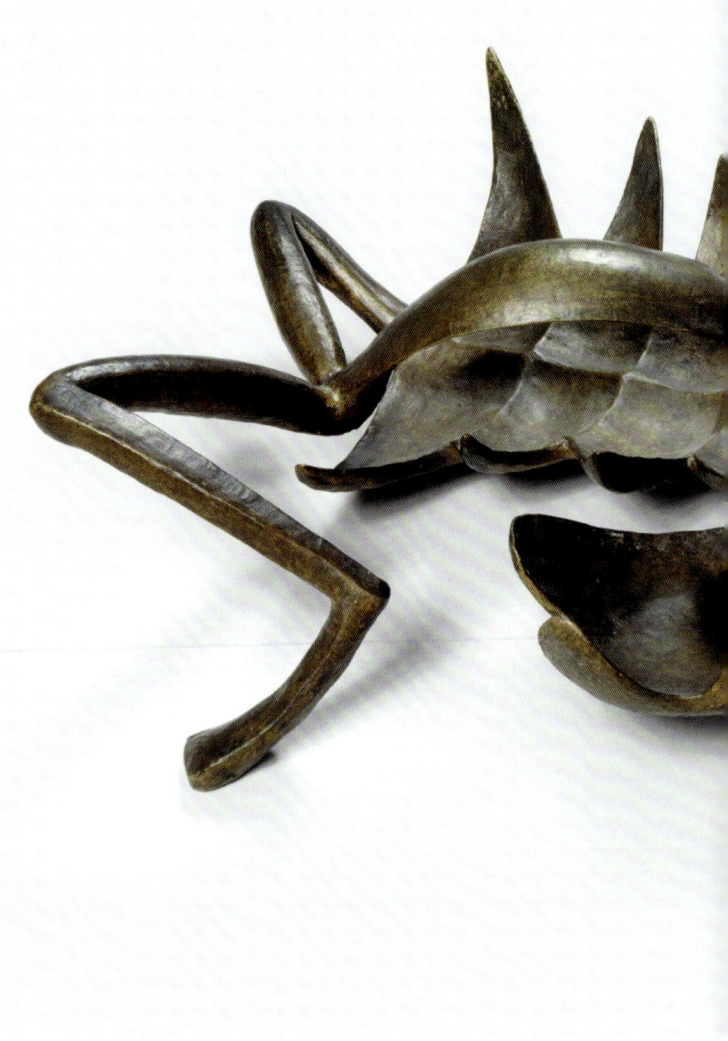

Woman with Her Throat Cut
1932
Bronze
22 × 75 × 58

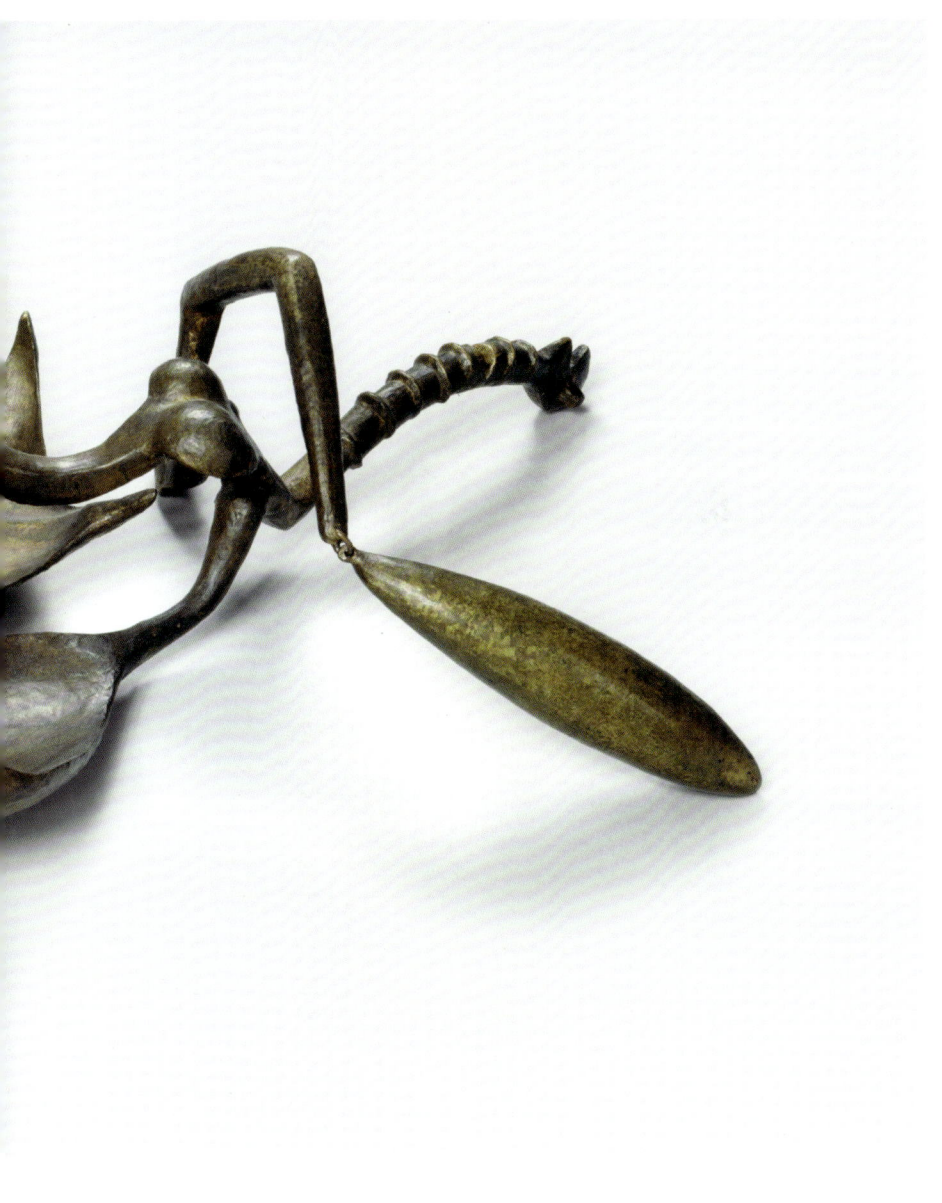

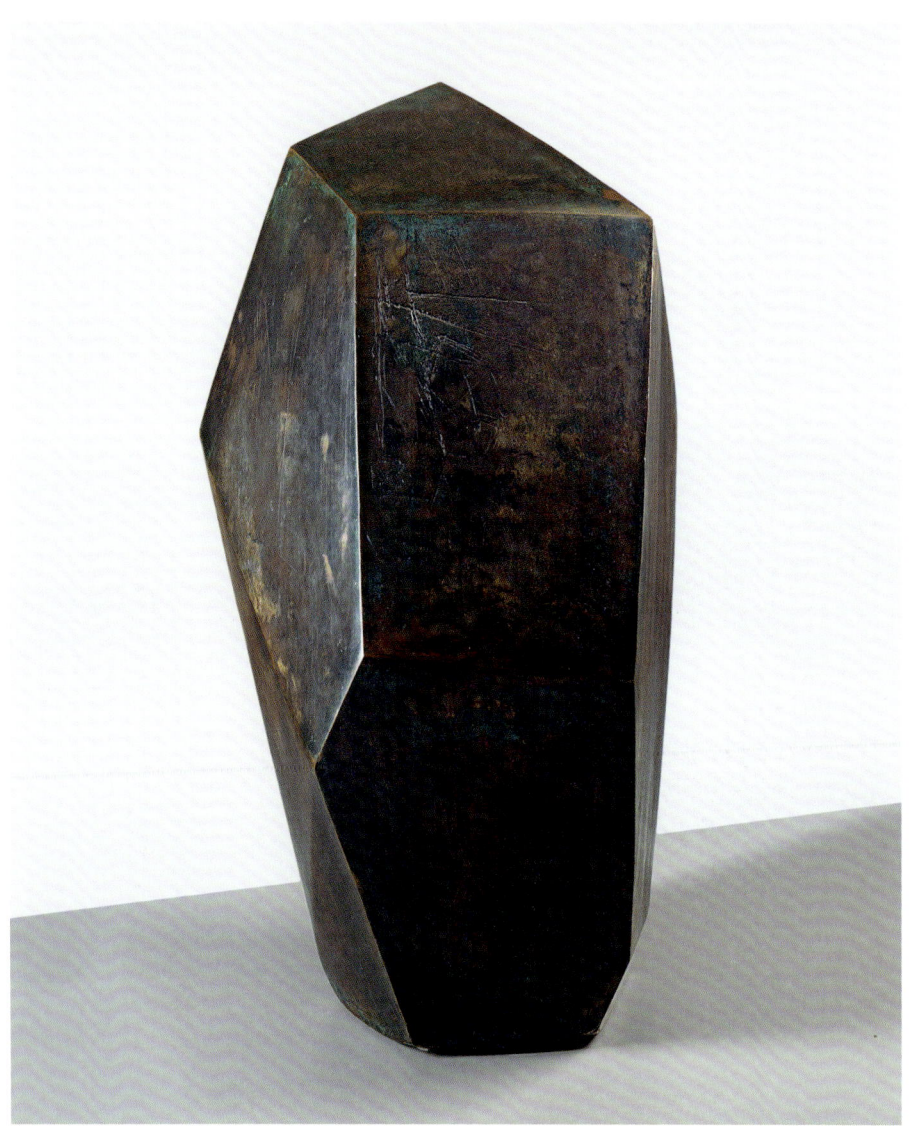

Cube 1933–4
Bronze
94.8 × 54 × 59

Table 1933
Plaster
148.5 × 103 × 43

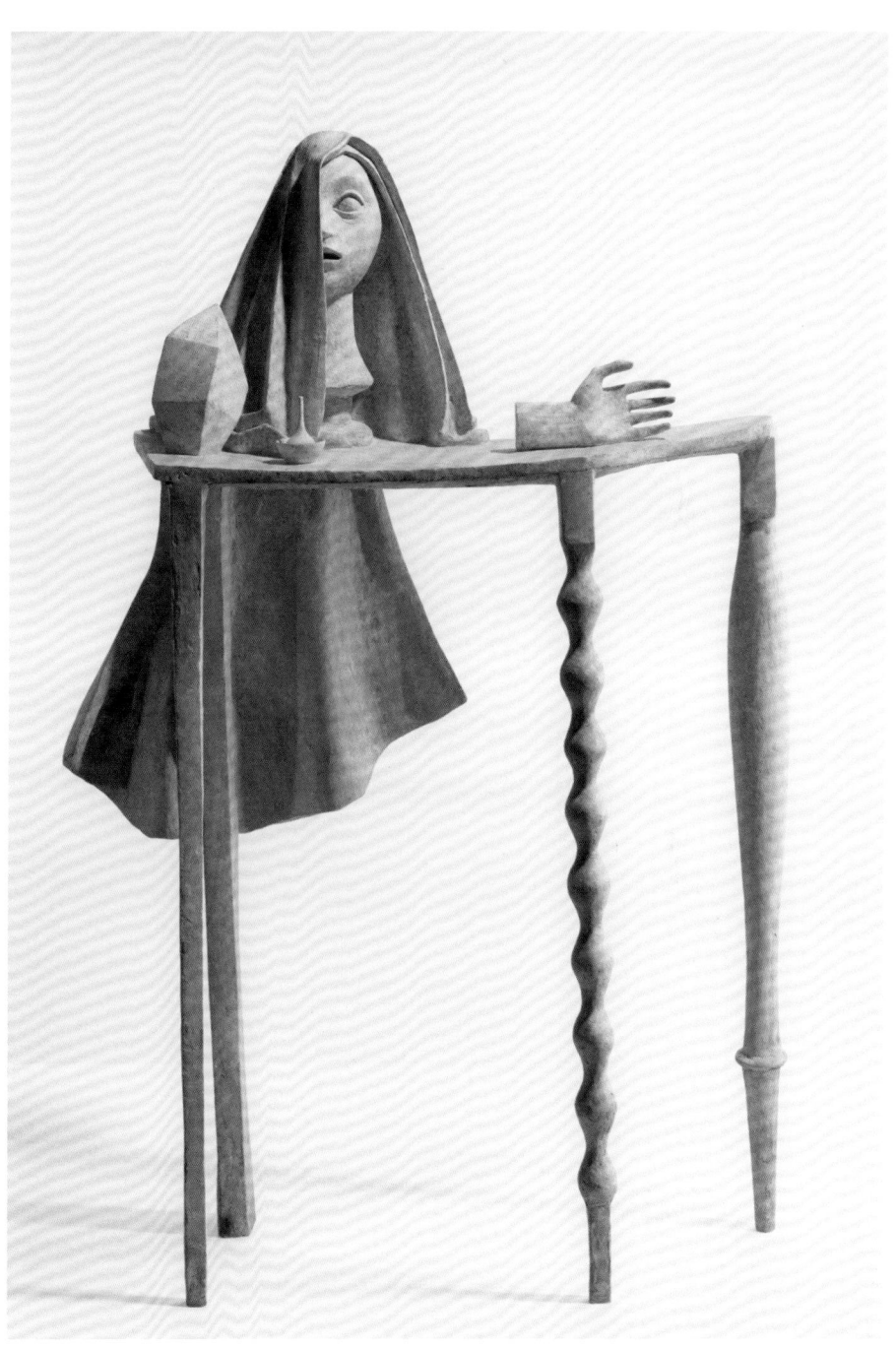

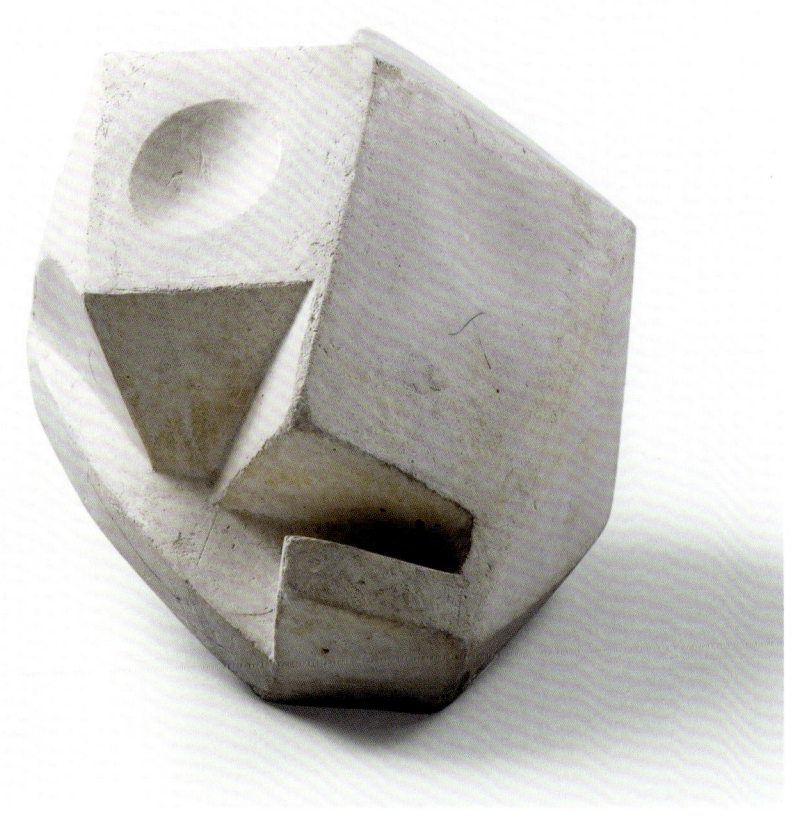

Head-Skull 1934
Plaster
18.4 × 19.9 × 22.3

Invisible Object 1934–5
Bronze
153 × 32 × 29

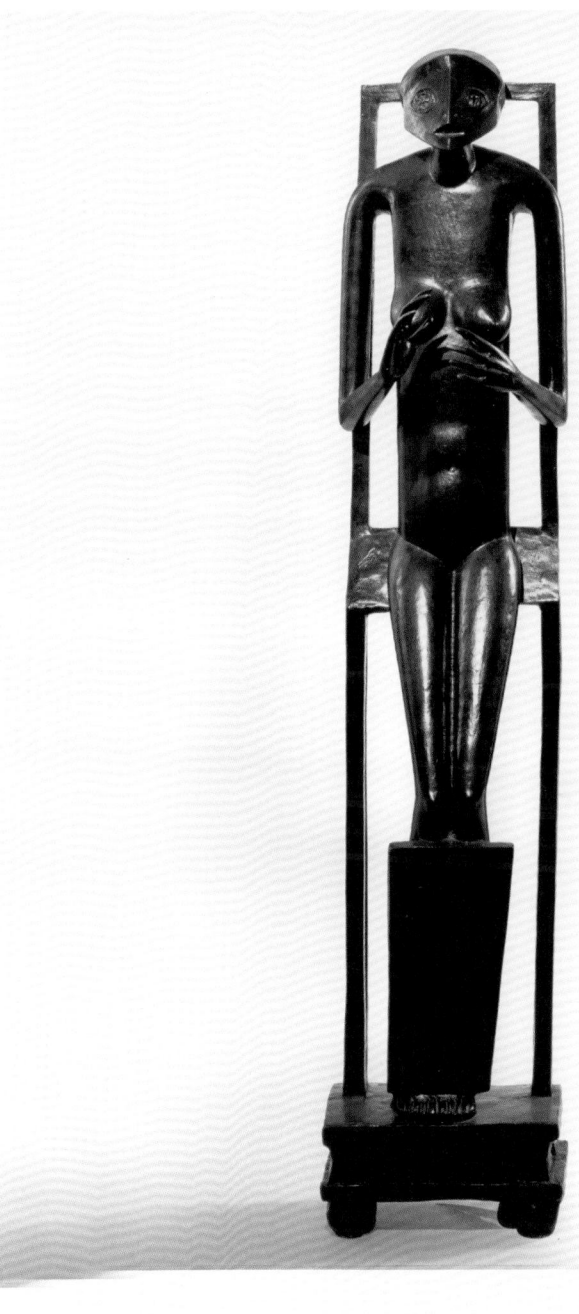

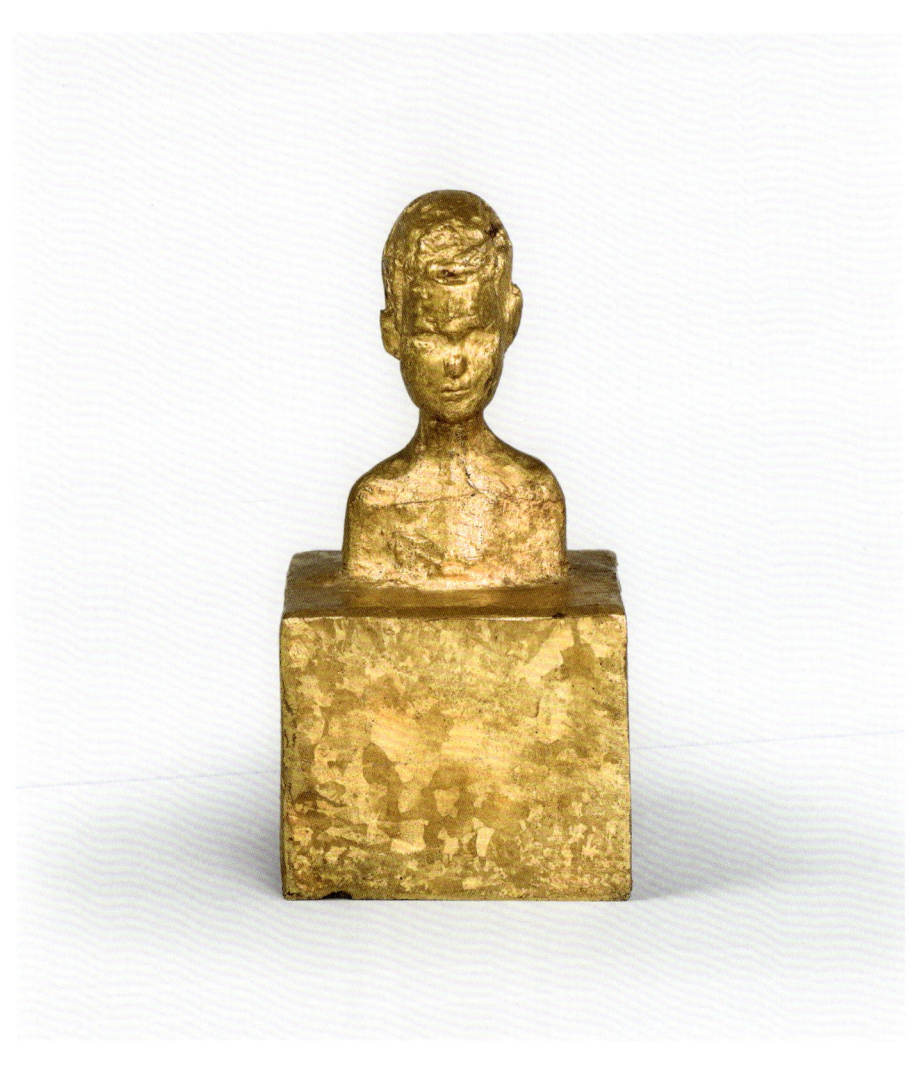

Small Bust of Silvio on a Base
1944–5
Bronze
11.2 × 5.6 × 6

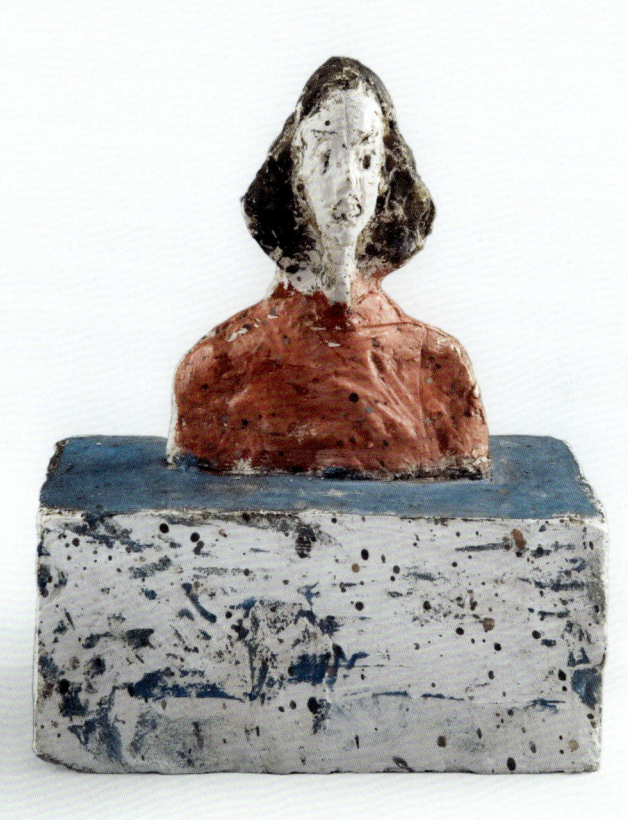

Small Bust of Annette 1946
Painted plaster
19 × 15.9 × 9.6

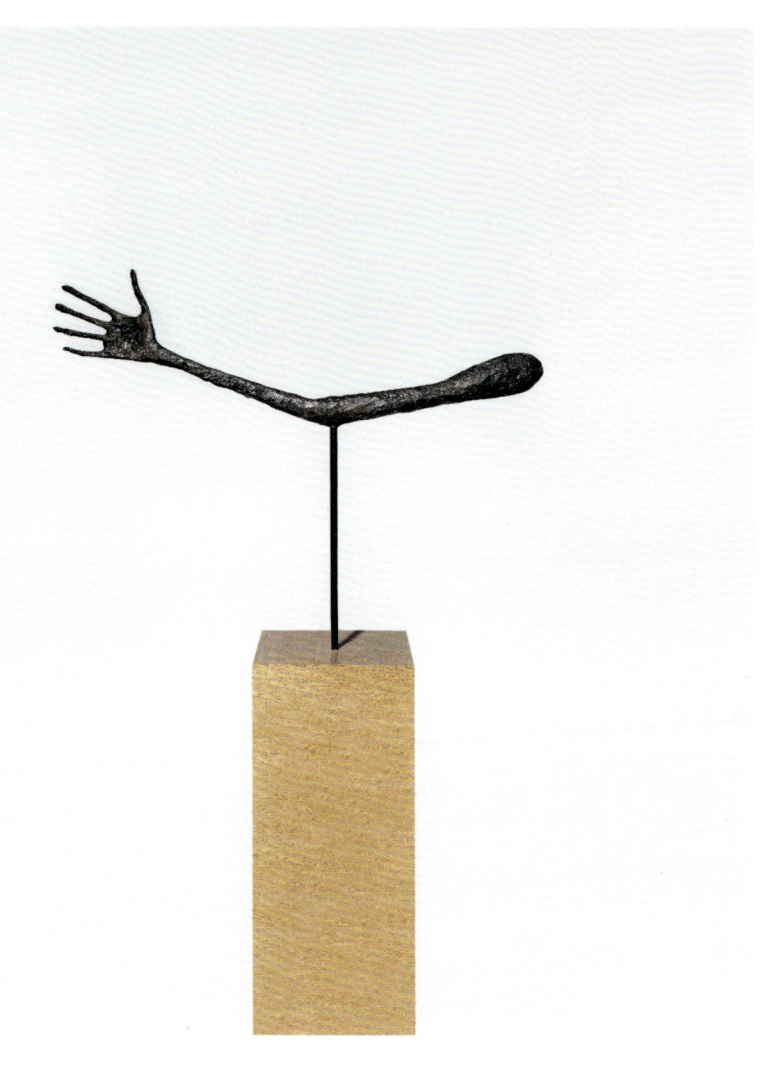

The Hand 1947
Bronze
57 × 72 × 3.5

Man Pointing 1947
Bronze
178 × 95 × 52

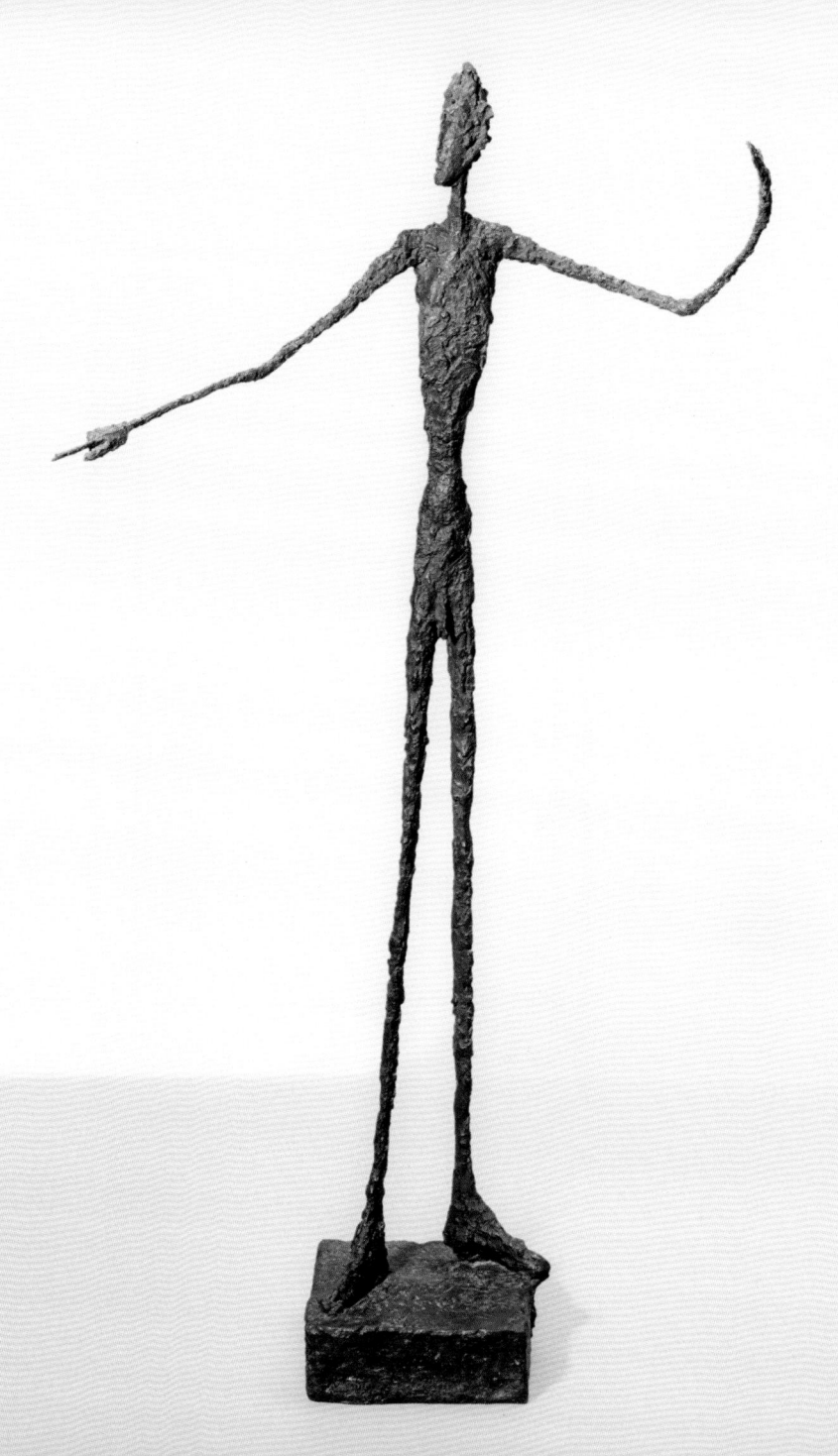

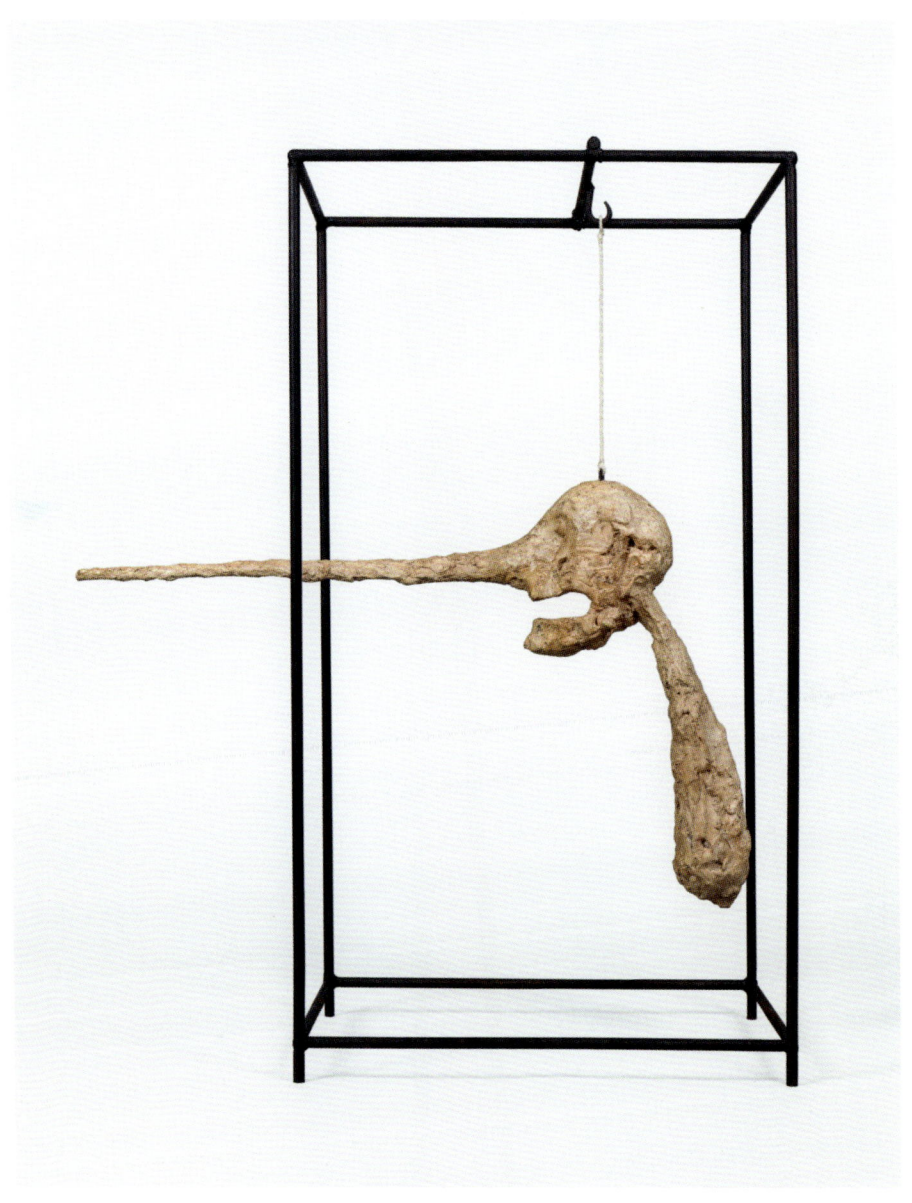

The Nose 1947
Plaster
43.6 × 9.2 × 61.6

Falling Man 1950
Bronze
47.5 × 13.5 × 12

OVERLEAF
The Square 1948
Bronze
20.8 × 63.5 × 43.6

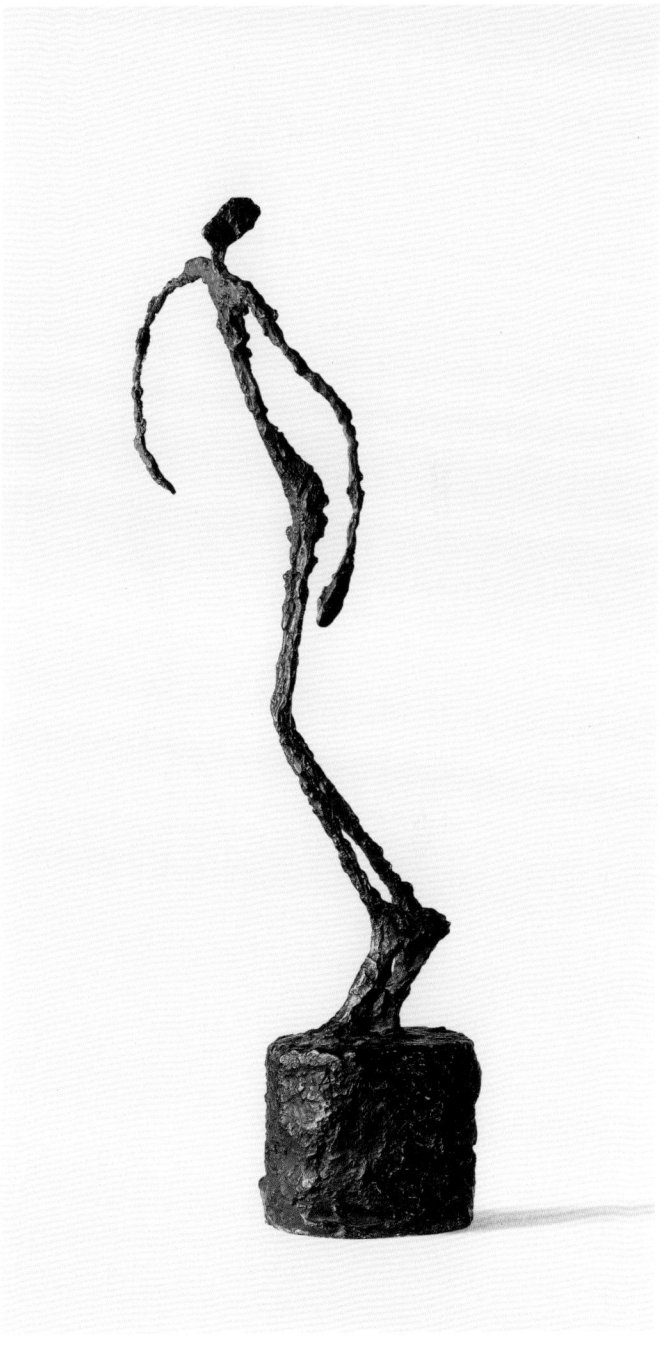

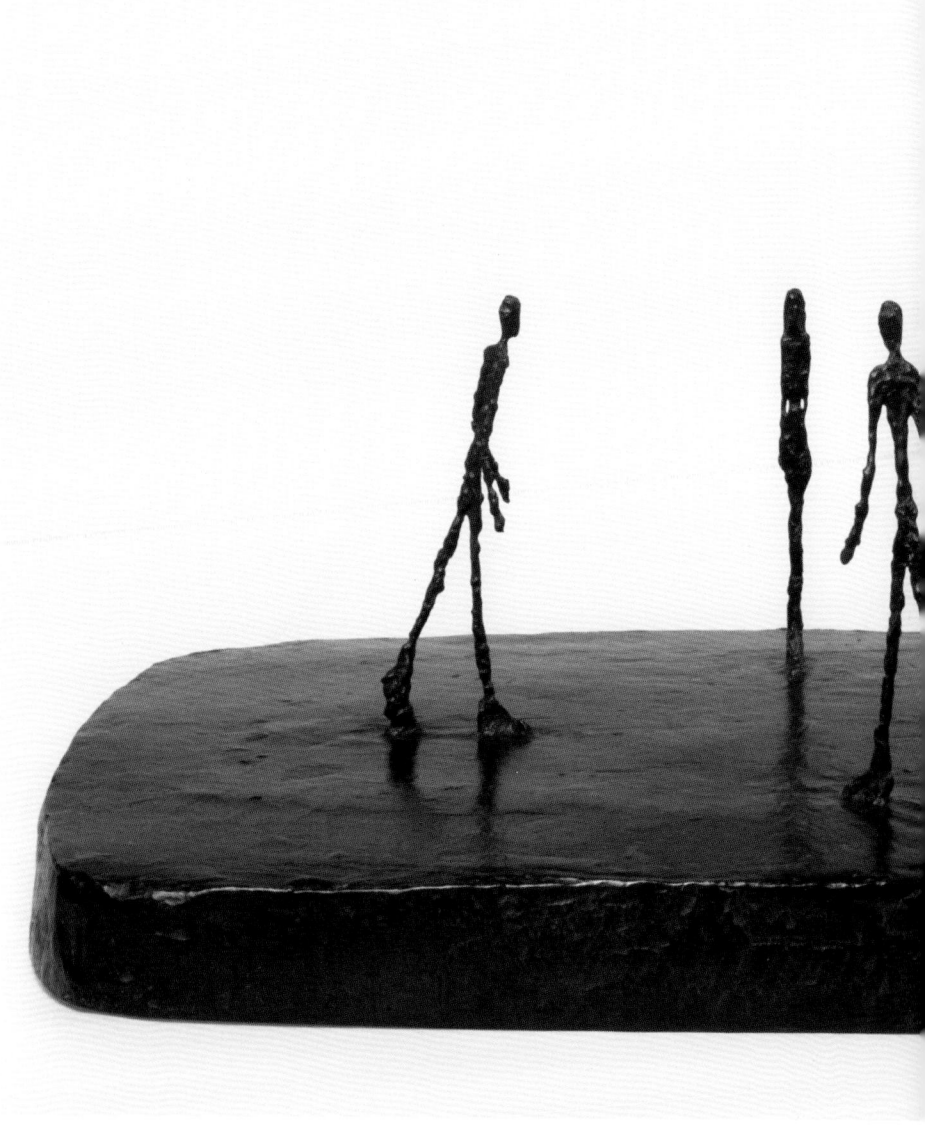

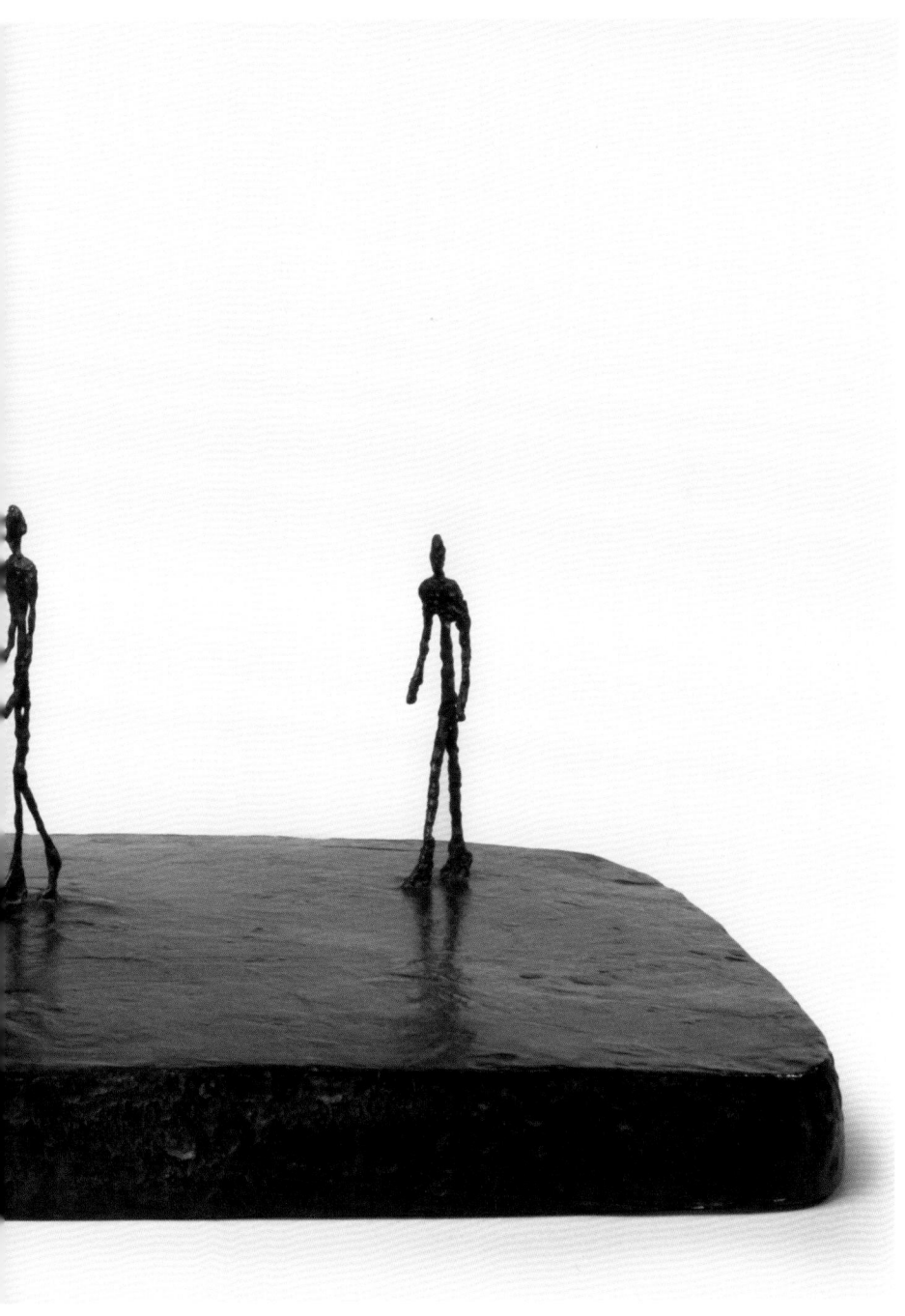

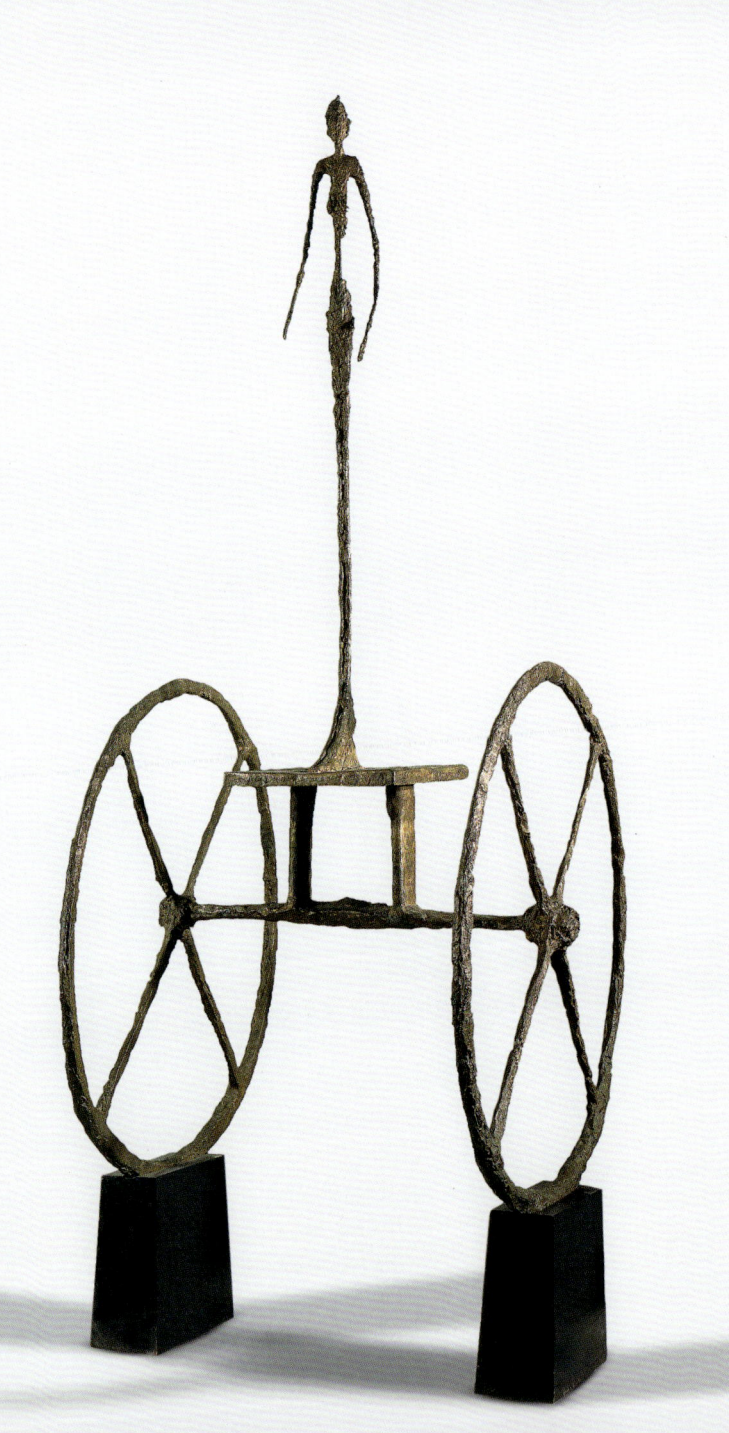

The Chariot 1950
Bronze
167 × 69 × 69

Woman of Venice V 1956
Painted plaster
113.5 × 14.5 × 31.8

OVERLEAF
The Dog 1951
Bronze
46 × 98.5 × 15

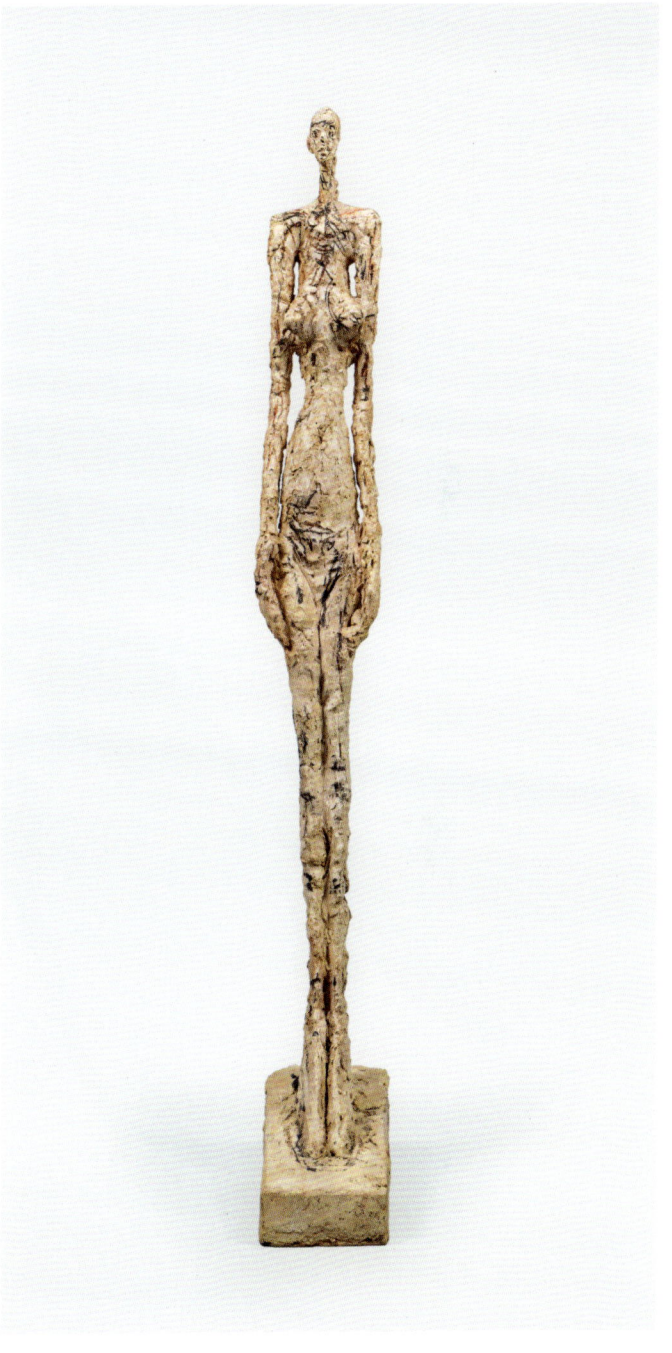

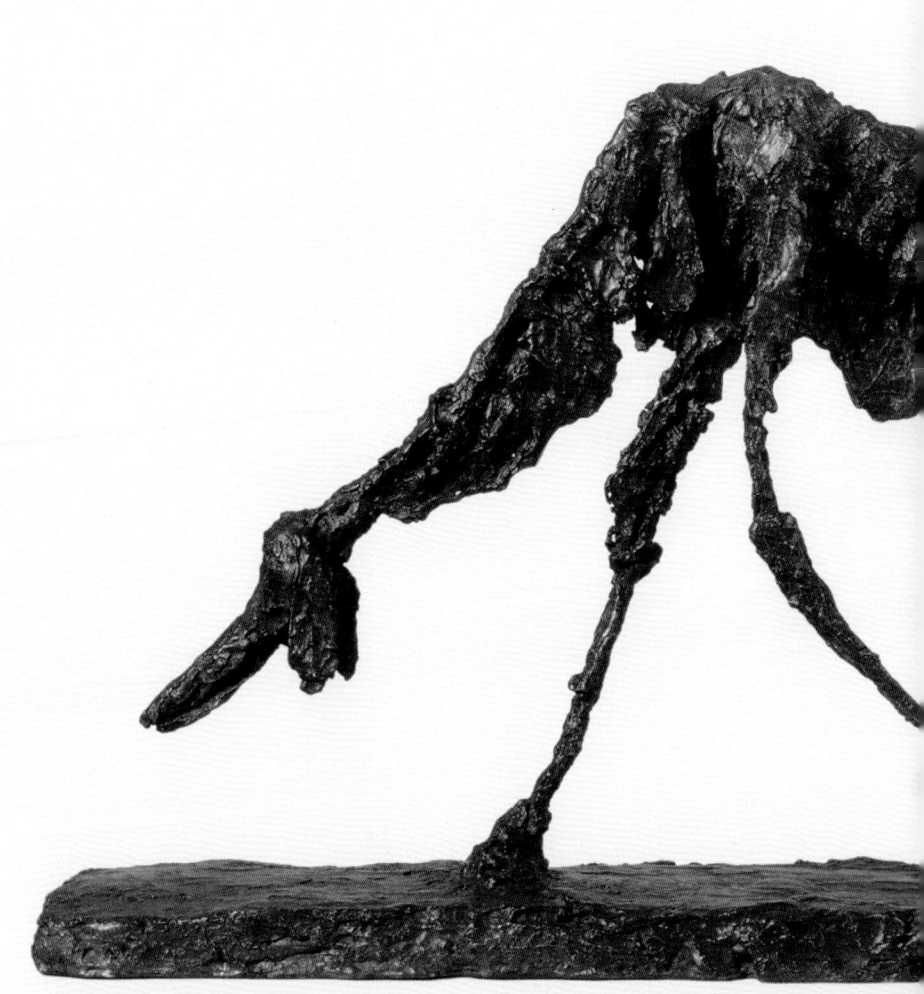

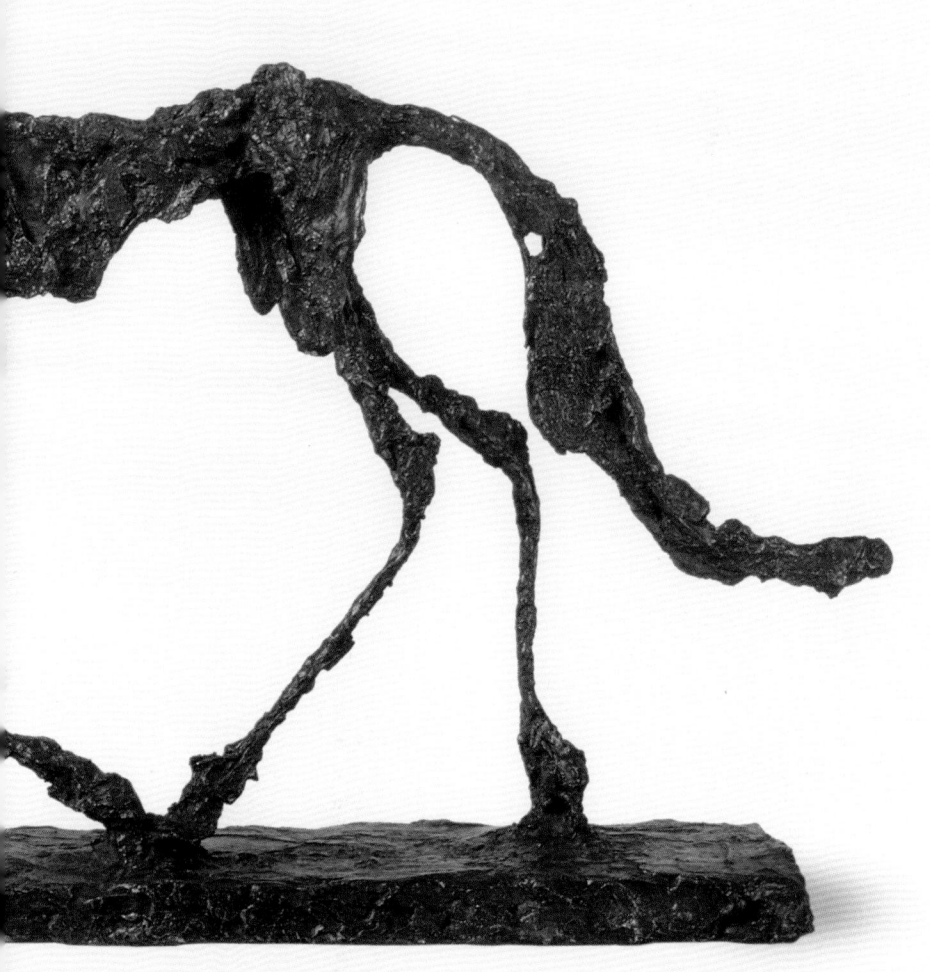

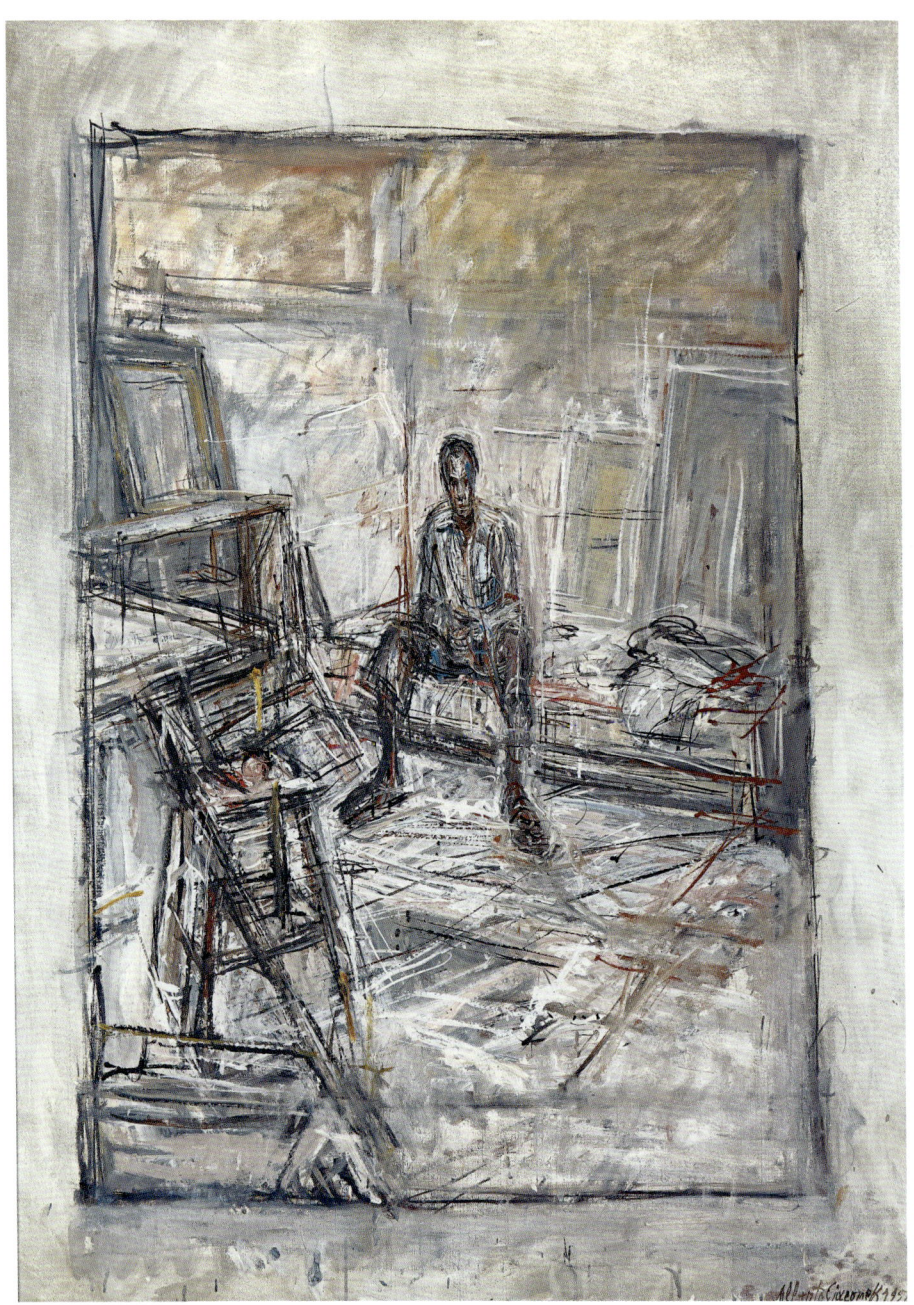

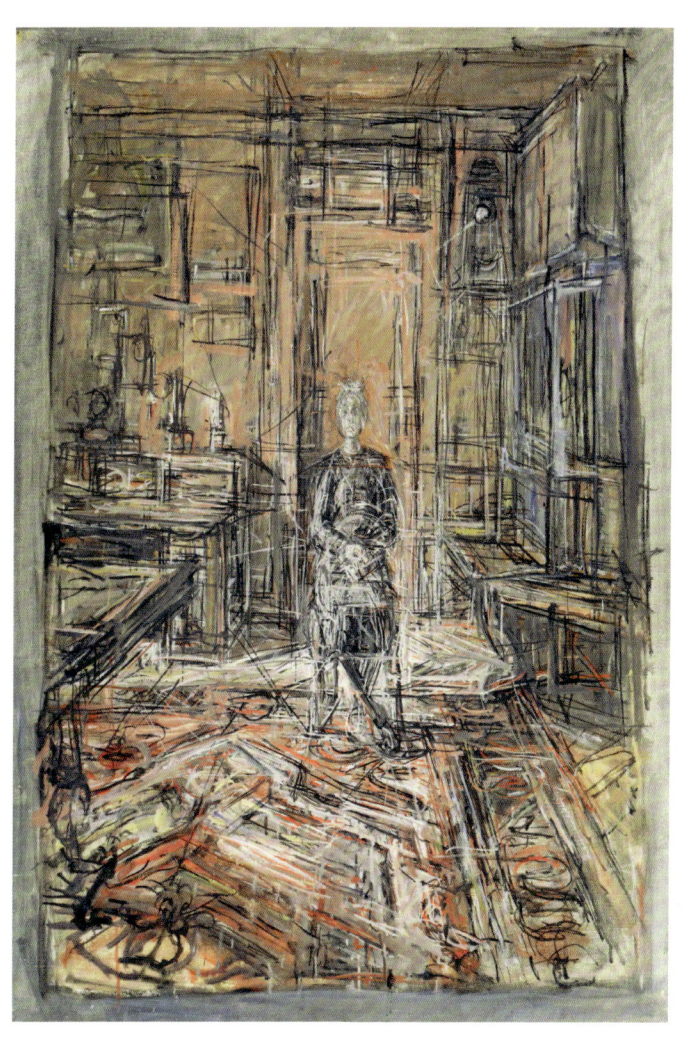

Diego 1950
Oil paint on canvas
80 × 58.4

The Artist's Mother 1950
Oil paint on canvas
89.9 × 61

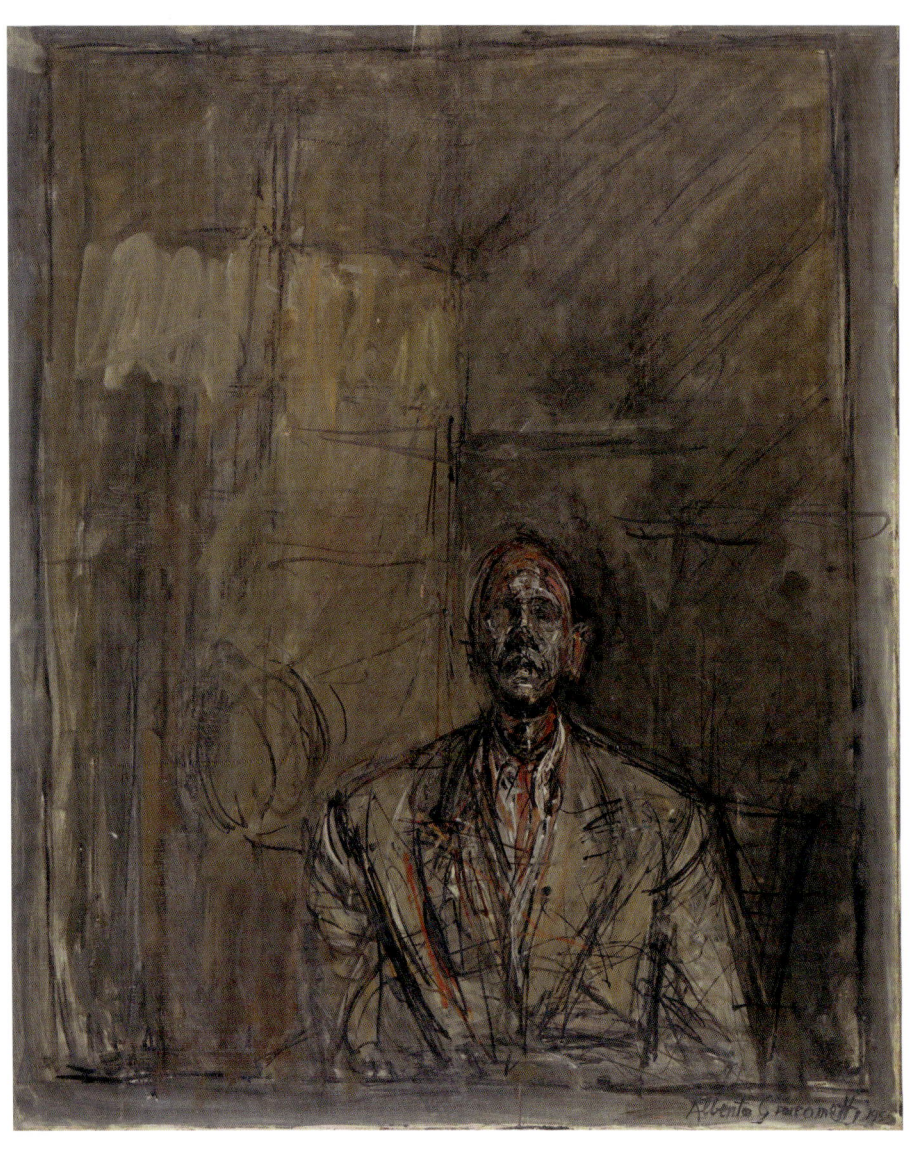

Jean Genet c.1954
Oil paint on canvas
65.3 × 54.3

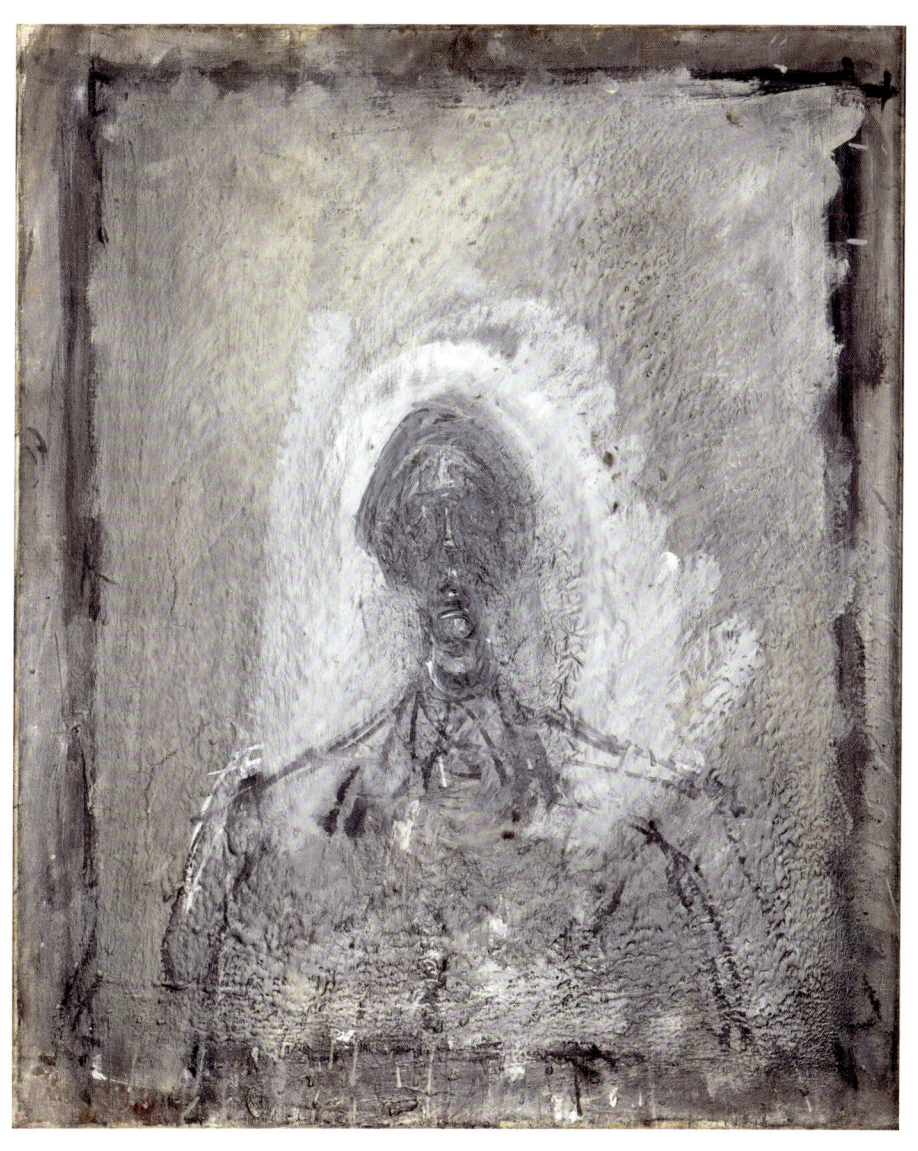

Bust of Yanaihara 1959
Oil paint on canvas
54.5 × 46.1

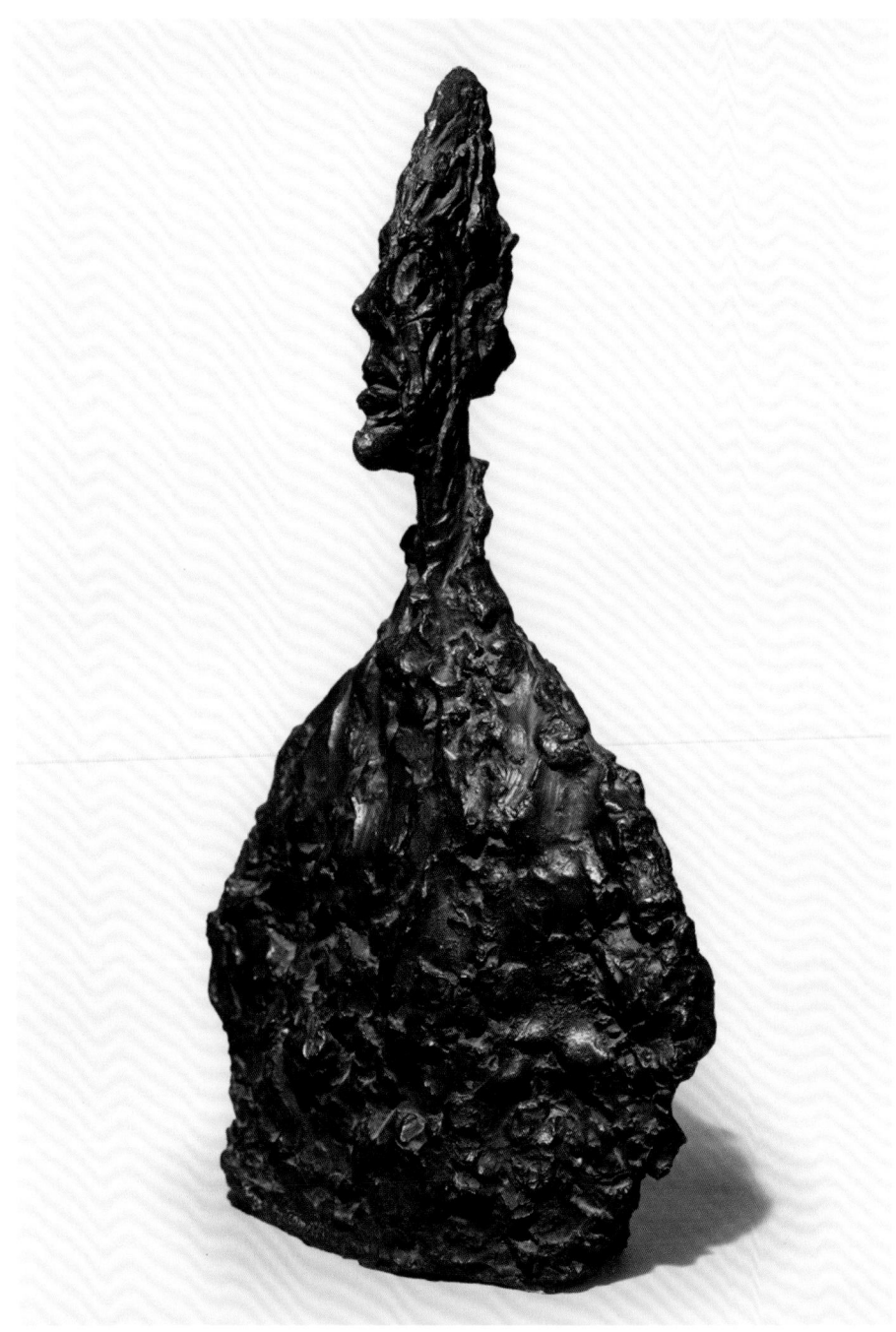

Bust of Diego 1955
Bronze
56.5 × 32 × 14.5

Standing Woman 1 1960
Bronze
272 × 34.9 × 54

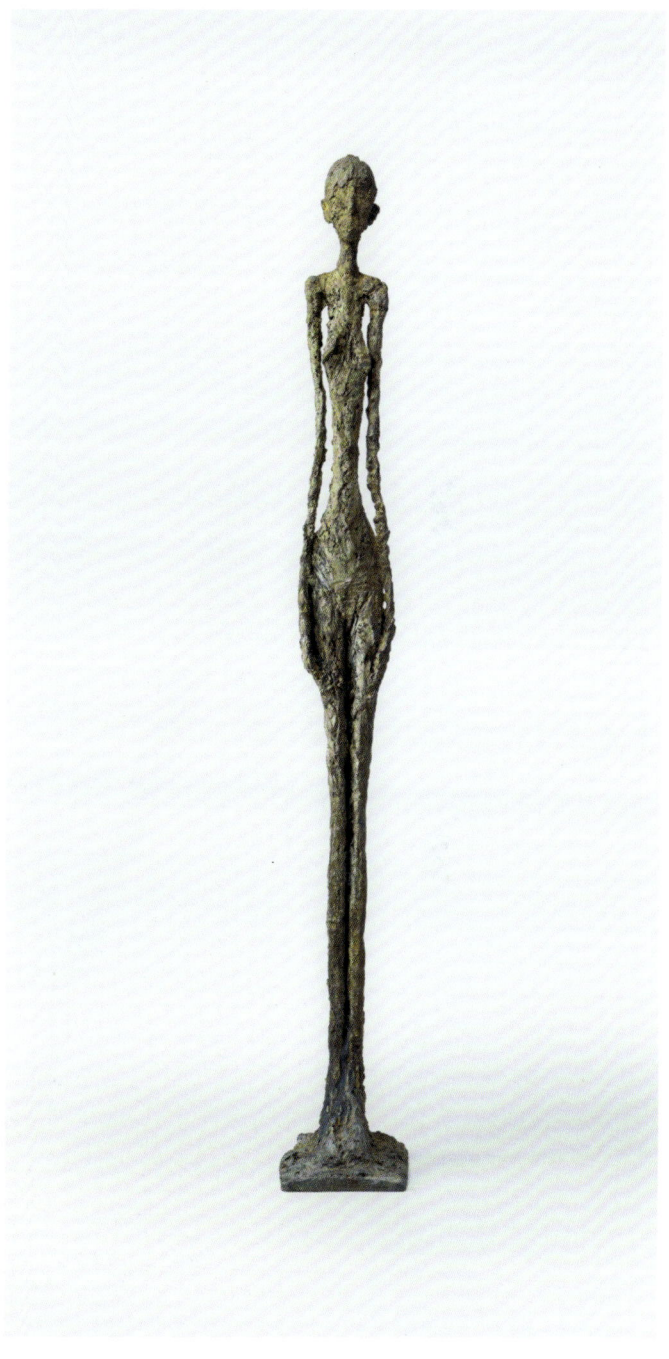

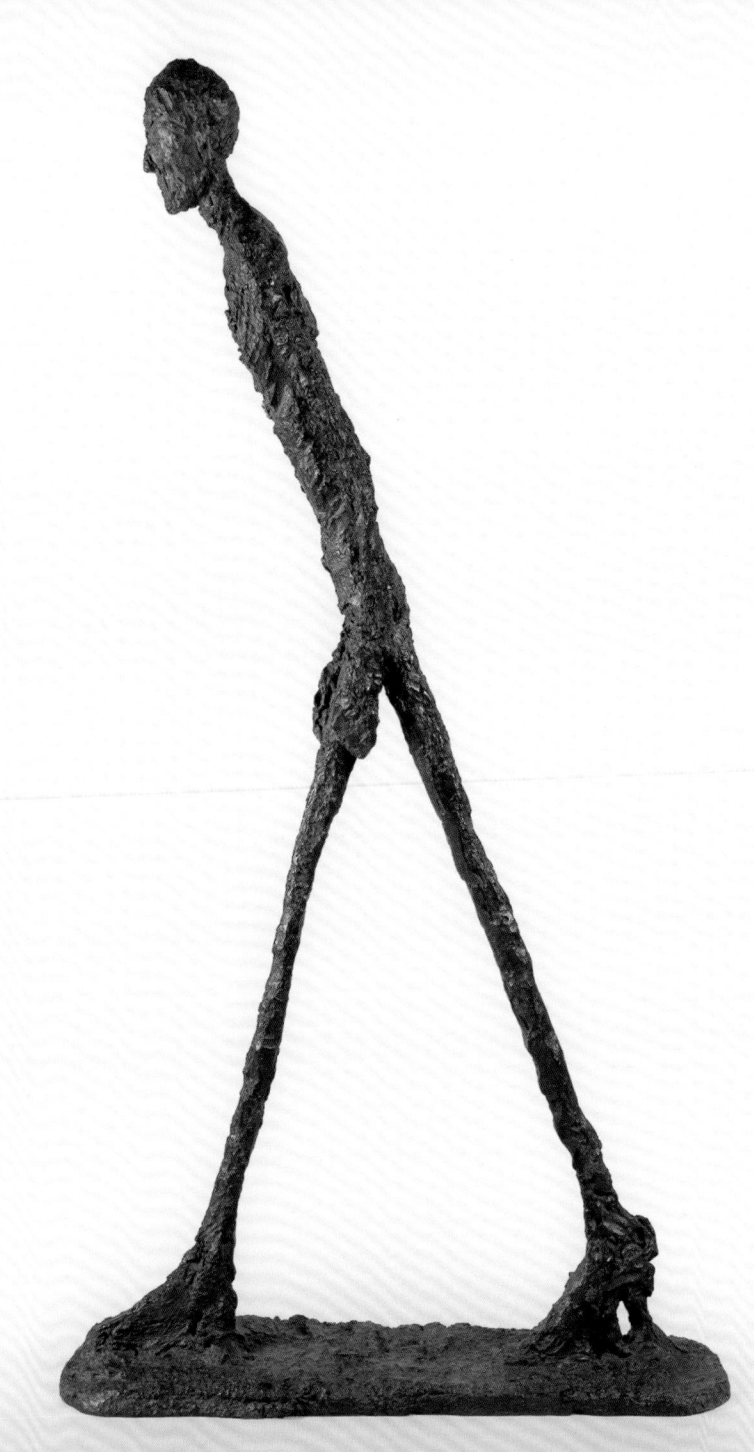

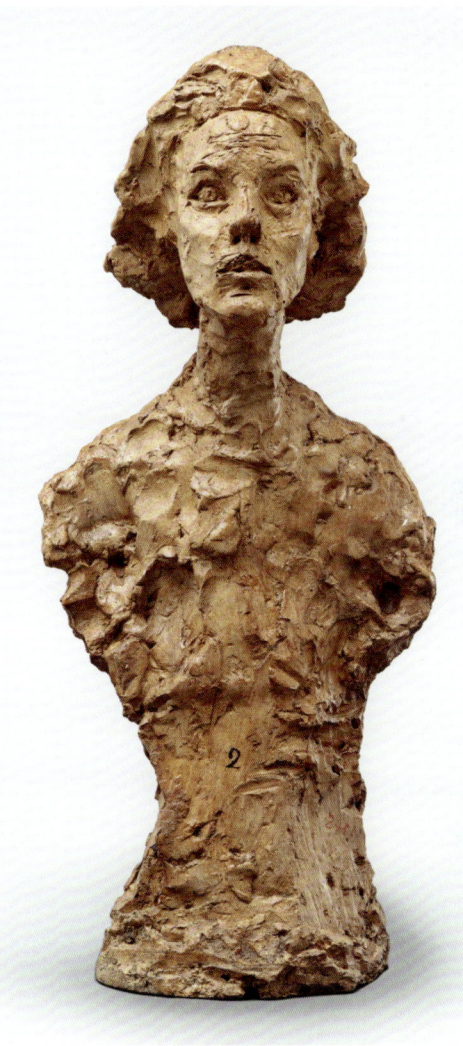

Walking Man I 1960
Bronze
180.5 × 27 × 97

Bust of Annette VIII 1962
Plaster
60.2 × 27.5 × 25.2

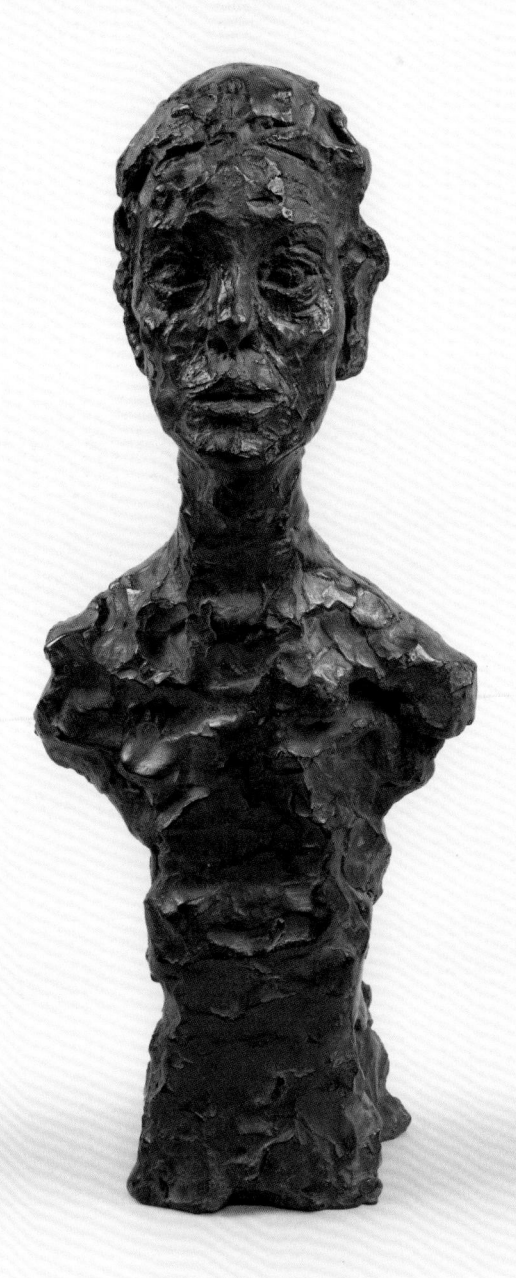

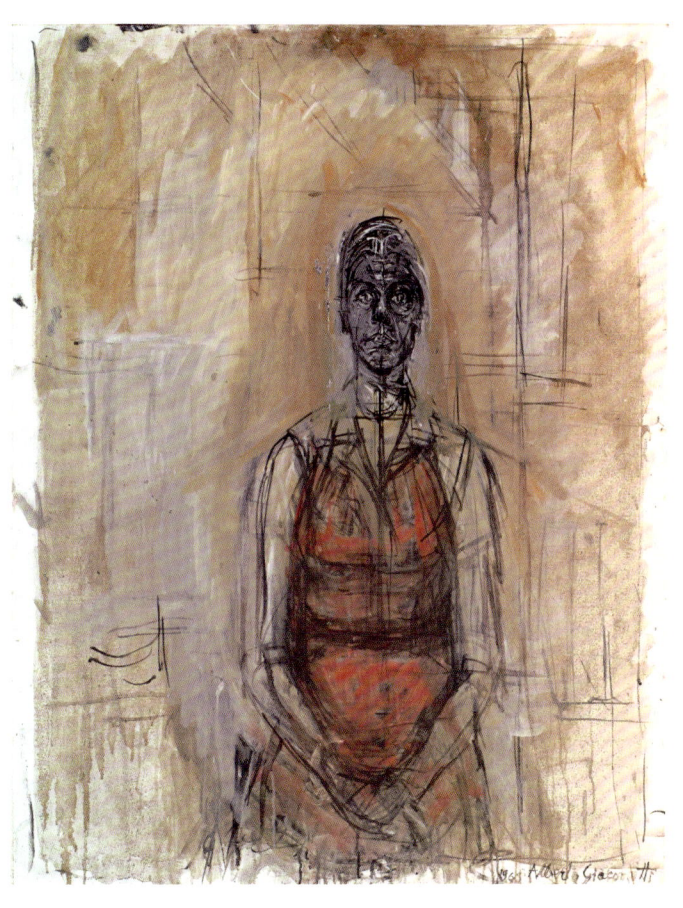

Bust of Annette X 1965
Bronze
45 × 18.5 × 13.4

Caroline 1965
Oil paint on canvas
92 × 73

NOTES

1. Letter from Alberto Giacometti to Peter F. Althaus, 1958, quoted in Reinhold Hohl, *Giacometti. A Biography in Pictures*, Ostfildern-Ruit 1998, p.13.

2. Letter from Giovanni Giacometti to Cuno Amiet, 25 October 1905, quoted in Centro Giacometti, *Das Atelier. Der Einzug der Familie Giacometti*, http://www.centrogiacometti.ch/de/der-ort/atelier-giacometti (accessed 8 August 2016), trans. Lena Fritsch.

3. Alberto Giacometti, 'Notes sur les copies', 30 November 1965, quoted in Alberto Giacometti, *Écrits: Articles, notes et entretiens*, Paris 2013, p.168, trans. Lena Fritsch.

4. Letter from Alberto Giacometti to Cuno Amiet, quoted in Hohl 1998, p.26.

5. Letter from Alberto Giacometti to Pierre Matisse, 1947, quoted in Luxembourg & Dayan, *Alberto Giacometti in his own Words*, London 2016, p.30, trans. Luxembourg & Dayan.

6. Letter from Alberto Giacometti to his parents, quoted in Hohl 1998, p.33.

7. Jean Clay, 'Alberto Giacometti: Le dialogue avec la mort d'un très grand sculpteur de notre temps', *Réalités*, no.215, December 1963, quoted in Hohl 1998, p.34.

8. Alberto Giacometti, 'Entretien avec André Parinaud', 1962, quoted in *Écrits* 2013, p.243, trans. Lena Fritsch.

9. Ibid.

10. Letter from Alberto Giacometti to Pierre Matisse, 1947, quoted in Luxembourg & Dayan 2016, p.31.

11. Georges Charbonnier, 'Entretien avec Alberto Giacometti', 1953, quoted in Hohl 1998, p.58.

12. This notebook is in the collection of the Fondation Giacometti, Paris.

13. Clay 1963, quoted in Hohl 1998, p.63.

14. Salvador Dalí, 'Objets à fonctionnement symbolique', *Le Surréalisme au service de la Révolution*, no.3, 1931, trans. Charles Penwarden. Dalí refers to the early version of the work, with a wooden ball.

15. Philosopher and art historian Georges Didi-Huberman has analysed the work in his book *Le Cube et le Visage. Autour d'une sculpture d'Alberto Giacometti*, Paris 1993.

16. 'Surrealist Art is Clumsy as well as Meaningless', *Evening News*, 12 June 1936, page number unknown.

17. Letter from Alberto Giacometti to Pierre Matisse, dated 3 November 1948, The Morgan Library & Museum, New York, Matisse Gallery Archives, Box 11, folder 8, item 43, trans. Charles Penwarden.

18. Letter from Jean-Michel Frank to Alberto Giacometti, c. October 1934, Fondation Giacometti, Paris, trans. Charles Penwarden.

19. Letter from Alberto Giacometti to Pierre Matisse, 1947, quoted in Luxembourg & Dayan 2016, p.32.

20. Alberto Giacometti, 'Entretien avec Pierre Dumayet', 1963, quoted in *Écrits* 2013, p.304, trans. Lena Fritsch.

21. Letter from Alberto Giacometti to Isabel Rawsthorne, 30 July 1945, Tate Archive (9612.1.2.5), trans. Lena Fritsch.

22. Alberto Giacometti in 1964, quoted in David Sylvester, *Looking at Giacometti*, London and New York 1997, p.6.

23. Jean-Paul Sartre, 'The Search for the Absolute', *Alberto Giacometti: Sculptures, Paintings, Drawings*, Pierre Matisse Gallery, New York 1948.

24. David Sylvester, 'Round the London Galleries', *The Listener*, 24 July 1952, p.159.

25. 'My Long March: An Interview with Pierre Schneider', originally published in *L'Express*, no.521, 8 June 1961, p.48, reprinted in Ángel González, *Alberto Giacometti: Works, Writings, Interviews*, Barcelona 2006, p.143.

26. Alberto Giacometti, 'Depuis 15 Jours', c.1952, quoted in *Écrits* 2013, p.318, trans. Lena Fritsch.

27. Alberto Giacometti in conversation with Gotthard Jedlicka, quoted in Hohl 1998, p.172.

28. Jean Genet, 'Alberto Giacometti's Studio', first published in *Derrière le miroir*, Paris 1957, quoted in Tate Gallery Liverpool, *Alberto Giacometti – The Artist's Studio*, London 1991, p.27, trans. Charles Penwarden.

29. Brassaï, *Brassaï. The Artists of My Life*, London 1982, p.54, trans. Richard Miller.

30. Ibid.

31. Alberto Giacometti in the documentary film Un homme parmi les hommes: Alberto Giacometti, directed by Jean-Marie Drot, Paris 1963, trans. Lena Fritsch.

32. Alberto Giacometti, quoted in Hohl 1998, p.166.

33. Ibid., p.169.

34. Letter from Alberto Giacometti to Norman Reid, 1 December 1965, Tate Archive.

35. Brassaï 1982, p.54.

36. Hohl 1998, p.195.

CREDITS

INDEX

Page references in *italics* indicate images.

First published 2017 by order of the Tate Trustees
by Tate Publishing, a division of Tate Enterprises
LTD Millbank, London SW1P 4RG
www.tate.org.uk

Reissued in 2025

THE AUTHOR
Dr Lena Fritsch is the Curator of Modern &
Contemporary Art at the Ashmolean Museum
and teaches at the University of Oxford. She was
previously at Tate Modern and co-curated the
gallery's major Giacometti retrospective in 2017.

Artworks on the following pages are from
Collection Fondation Giacometti, Paris 4, 8, 11, 17,
19, 25, 32, 34–9, 43, 52, 54, 55, 58, 63, 69, 72 and 74

A catalogue record for this book is available from
the British Library

ISBN 978 1 84976 993 8

Distributed in the United States and Canada by
ABRAMS, New York

Library of Congress Control Number applied for

Commissioning Editor: Emma Poulter
Project Editor: Aki Gurung
Production: Juliette Dupire
Picture Research: Bill Jones
Designed by Astrid Stavro Studio
Colour reproduction by DL Imaging, London
Printed and bound in Italy by Printer Trento, S.r.l.

Cover: Alberto Giacometti, The Square 1948 (detail,
see pp.60–1)
Frontispiece: Alberto Giacometti, The Artist's Mother
1950 (detail, see p.67)

Measurements of artworks are given in
centimetres, height before width and depth

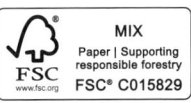

FSC
www.fsc.org
MIX
Paper | Supporting
responsible forestry
FSC® C015829